D1524730

The Changing Structure of Labour in Japan

The Changing Structure of Labour in Japan

Japanese Human Resource
Management: between Continuity
and Innovation

Edited by

René Haak

First published 2006 by
PALGRAVE MACMILLAN
Houndmills, Basingstoke, Hampshire RG21 6XS and
175 Fifth Avenue, New York, N.Y. 10010
Companies and representatives throughout the world

PALGRAVE MACMILLAN is the global academic imprint of the Palgrave
Macmillan division of St. Martin's Press, LLC and of Palgrave Macmillan Ltd.
Macmillan® is a registered trademark in the United States, United Kingdom
and other countries. Palgrave is a registered trademark in the European
Union and other countries.

ISBN-13: 978–1–4039–4292–0
ISBN-10: 1–4039–4292–7

This book is printed on paper suitable for recycling and made from fully
managed and sustained forest sources.

A catalogue record for this book is available from the British Library.

Library of Congress Cataloging-in-Publication Data
    The changing structure of labour in Japan : Japanese human
resource management: between continuity and innovation / edited by
René Haak.
        p. cm.
    Includes bibliographical references and index.
    ISBN 1–4039–4292–7 (alk. paper)
        1. Personnel management – Japan. 2. Industrial management –
Japan. I. Haak, René.
HF5549.2.J3C44 2005
658.3'00952—dc22   2005051554

10 9 8 7 6 5 4 3 2 1
15 14 13 12 11 10 09 08 07 06

Printed and bound in Great Britain by
Antony Rowe Ltd, Chippenham and Eastbourne

Contents

List of Figures

List of Tables

Foreword

For a little more than a decade Japan has been in the grip of far-reaching structural reforms. Since it became clear, in the early 1990s, that the 'bubble era' had come to an end for good the rhetoric of deregulation and reform has swept every arena of government, economy and society. And it wasn't just rhetoric. The decade around the turn of the century saw real changes and transformations in Japan some of which many observers would not have thought possible just a decade earlier. The Japanese labour market is one of the arenas where change is most conspicuous.

The 'three pillars' of Japanese capitalism, lifetime employment, seniority wages and enterprise unions, have come under serious pressure, while the one-income family model is giving way to a pattern where in excess of 60 percent of all households rely on two incomes. Unemployment, unknown to an entire generation of Japanese workers, has become a problem, and the market for temporary labour has expanded significantly and rapidly. Although lifetime employment in a big firm is still aspired to by many, a decreasing number of actual career prospects offer this option.

At present, the labour market and the society at large are characterized by a great deal of uncertainty and volatility. Reforms continue, while new models of employment and compensation are being put to the test. A new system of industrial relations is evolving moving away from the old qualification-based system that stressed accumulation and improvement of human capital and was so successful during the high-growth period, to a more performance oriented system. Much is in flux, and any attempt to delineate the future shape of Japanese industrial relations would be premature, but it is quite obvious that these relations will never again be what they were from the late 1960s to the early 1990s when the Japanese corporation was regarded as a model to emulate by managers around the globe. Under the influence of globalizing markets, new technologies and population ageing, human resource management has to adjust to changing frame conditions. The adjustments have not been completed.

The German Institute for Japanese Studies (DIJ) is observing the ongoing changes in this area of the Japanese economy with keen interest. The present volume is a result of these efforts. It addresses the most relevant issues in human resource management with a view on how they are affected by the need of Japanese companies to improve their competitiveness in the world market. It includes in-depth analyses of organizational structure, compensation systems, qualifications, working time, and employment practices. Offering a comprehensive up-to date overview of Japanese human resource management by internationally renowned experts in the field, it contributes to our understanding of the complex process in the course of which Japan Inc. is reinventing itself.

FLORIAN COULMAS

Tokyo   *Director, German Institute for Japanese Studies*

Notes on the Contributors

Eileen Appelbaum is Director of the Center for Women and Work, Rutgers University, USA.

Tom Bailey is Director of the Institute on Education and Economy, Teachers College, Columbia University, USA.

John Benson is Professor of Management and Chair, MBA Program in International Business University of Tsukuba, Tokyo, Japan.

Peter Berg is an Associate Professor at the School of Labor and Industrial Relations, Michigan State University, USA.

Florian Coulmas is Director of the German Institute for Japanese Studies, Tokyo, Japan.

Philippe Debroux is a Professor at Soka University, Tokyo, Japan.

Markus Falk is Director of Human Resources, BASF South East Asia Regional Headquarters, Singapore (he worked in BASF Japan as General Manager HR from 2001 to 2003).

Hiroyuki Fujimura is an Associate Professor at the Faculty of Business Administration, Human Resource Development, Hosei University, Tokyo, Japan.

René Haak is Head of the Business and Economics Section and Deputy Director of the German Institute for Japanese Studies, Tokyo, Japan.

Tadashi Hanami is Professor Emeritus at Sophia University, Special Advisor to the Minister in charge of Civil Service Reform, and former Director of the The Japan Institute of Labor, Tokyo, Japan.

Jun Imai is a Research Associate at the University of Duisburg-Essen, Germany, and a PhD candidate at the State University of New York, Stony Brook, USA.

Arne L. Kalleberg is Professor of Sociology at the University of North Carolina, Chapel Hill, USA.

David Methé is an Associate Professor at the Institute of Business and Accounting, Kwansei Gakuin University, Japan.

Junichiro Miyabe is an Associate Professor at Hokkaido University, Japan.

Michio Nitta is Professor of the Institute of Social Science, University of Tokyo, Japan.

Markus Pudelko is a Lecturer at the University of Edinburgh Management School, Edinburgh, United Kingdom.

Frank Schulz is a Senior Consultant at Transearch International Inc., Tokyo, Japan.

Karen Shire is a Professor of Sociology at the University of Essen-Duisburg, Germany.

Hiromasa Suzuki is a Professor at Waseda University, Tokyo, Japan.

Mahito Yamao is Director of Human Resources at BASF Japan.

1
Introduction: A View on Japanese Human Resource Management

René Haak

It cannot be disputed that after the wholescale devastation of the war years the Japanese achieved an extraordinary feat of economic and technological revival: growth rates averaged 10 per cent or higher during the period of dynamic growth between 1955 and the early 1970s. At the beginning of the 1980s – when the global success of some Japanese companies could no longer be ignored and US companies in particular were finding Japanese competition a challenge – works such as *Managing our Way to Industrial Decline* (Hayes and Abernathy, 1980) and *The New Industrial Competition* (Abernathy *et al.*, 1981) defined the tone of the discussion. The success of Japanese companies was seen not as an opportunity but as a threat, or at best as a challenge. Meeting this challenge was the only way in which other countries and companies could maintain their traditional leadership position (Chandler, 1992). Since then there have been numerous analyses of what made Japanese companies so competitive, and of how they developed new products, penetrated markets, organized industrial production and ensured the quality of their products.

The success of Japanese companies also presented a theoretical challenge as it was obvious that the existing management theories could not adequately explain this success. Japan's lack of raw materials and shortage of land did not seem conducive to competitiveness, but in fact proved to be beneficial as the Japanese were forced to concentrate on high-tech industries and rationalize the production processes in almost all areas of industry (Porter, 1990). Johnson (1982) gives a very detailed description of the part played by the state in the development of the Japanese economy. The Ministry of International Trade and Industry (MITI, now the Ministry of Economy, Trade and Industry METI) was highly significant in this regard, and particularly in respect of the support and coordination of basic research. However Porter (1990) notes that the part played by MITI in the 1980s should not be overestimated as most research was carried out in corporate R&D departments and was by no means open to all and sundry.

The network structure of Japanese companies has also been put forward as a central factor in their success (Imai, 1989; Odagiri, 1992; Sydow 1992). Indeed for Chandler (1990, 1992), this structure was so central that the Japanese economy could be viewed as 'group enterprise capitalism'. Building on Chandler's work, Suzuki (1991) described how Japanese companies developed and gained strength by internalizing human resource development. At the beginning of the twentieth century textile, mechanical engineering and metal processing firms were finding it very difficult to find suitably qualified personnel and keep them with the company, and therefore set up internal training schemes and developed a payment system based on length of service. Odagiri's (1992) analysis, which is based on Penrose's (1959) resource-oriented view, also highlights human resources and the importance of lifetime employment to corporate success. According to Odagiri there are two aspects to this: the strong growth orientation of Japanese companies, and the intense competition in all markets. He explains that a preference for strong growth was quite natural and that in the long term lifetime employment went hand in hand with good profit opportunities, more interesting work and more career options. However the goal of strong growth also encouraged direct competition between companies. While, moving between companies was not easy as individuals were bound to the company, this was conducive to internal competition between employees. All this had a positive impact on market structures, economic stability and growth, technical progress, international competitiveness, and macroeconomic structures, which in turn benefited human and financial resources. Although Odagiri's analysis adequately explains some aspects of Japanese corporate success, it is problematic in its overemphasis of the human resource argument and the simultaneous devaluation of the influence of investors.

Aoki (1989) subjects the human resource and capital factors to close scrutiny and concludes that it is mistaken to place excessive value on human resource management when explaining the success of Japanese companies. Aoki (2000) identifies two ways in which to run a company successfully. He considers that the key to Japanese corporate success (J-type) is the combination of intensive horizontal information flows with vertically oriented control of promotion and employees. The free flow of information in Japanese companies, which has considerable benefits for their development, is facilitated by vertical control. American companies (A-type) solve the problem of coordinating the exchange of information and personnel incentives in a different way. They combine a horizontally open personnel system, which includes strong specialization and uses external labour markets to manage careers. There is relatively rigid separation of the vertically oriented information channels. Aoki considers that both systems can be successful in their own way and refers to the principle of dualism in this context. The environmental circumstances dictate which type is likely to be preferred. Aoki discusses the degree of uncertainty in the corporate environment and concludes that when there is very low or very high uncertainty the hierarchical US model is more likely to be successful. With medium degrees of uncertainty the Japanese model is more likely to be effective. Aoki (1994) traces the success of Japanese companies in the processing and assembly industries – automotive, electronics and so on – back to this assumption and compares them to the advantages of the US model in aviation and chemicals. Communication, information and personnel incentive schemes are central pillars of his explanation. We shall not go into further detail about Aoki's analyses, which deal with agency theory and modern game theory, rather it suffices to say that human resource management has played a very crucial part in the success of Japanese companies.

One of the most influential works on human resource management is Ouchi's (1981) Theory Z, which can be seen as a continuation of McGregor's (1960) work on Theory X and Theory Y. According to McGregor, all management decisions are based on a series of hypotheses about human nature and human behaviour. He groups the assumptions made in traditional management methods under Theory X and puts them up against Theory Y as an ideal. Theory X assumes that humans have an innate aversion to work, and try to avoid it as much as possible. Accordingly most people have to be monitored, led and forced under threat of punishment to make a productive contribution to the achievement of the organization's goals. Theory X is therefore based on the assumption that humans like to be led, avoid responsibility, have little ambition and want security above all else.

Conversely, the most important assumption in Theory Y is that people do not have an innate aversion to work. Instead work is seen as an important source of satisfaction. If a person identifies with the goals of the organization it is unnecessary for management to exert control or for organizational structures to be imposed. Employees will develop self-control and initiative, and thus make a better contribution to the achievement of the company's goals. According to Theory Y, the most important incentives to work are to satisfy 'I-needs' and to bring about self-realization. Theory Y also assumes that humans seek responsibility, with appropriate guidance, and that resourcefulness and creativity on the part of employees are not exceptional but widespread, but are rarely stimulated in most industrial operations.

McGregor, building on Maslow's (1954) hypothesis that human needs are arranged hierarchically, does not consider that human need and motivation to contribute to the industrial labour process are reduced to the satisfaction of material requirements (as assumed in Theory X) but rather to satisfying social and ideal requirements (as assumed in Theory Y). Although McGregor's statement cannot be supported in this general, undifferentiated form and he also fails to specify the conditions under which the assumptions of Theories X and Y can claim validity, his simplified description of the dualistic approach is very accessible.

Ouchi (1981) has used this dualistic comparison to present his normative model of management, which he bases on in-depth comparisons of the US and Japanese management models. Ouchi assumes that society and organizations in North America and Japan differ significantly. He describes the cultural environment in the United States as heterogeneous, mobile and oriented towards the individual. Japanese society, on the other hand, is characterized as homogeneous, stable and collectivist. Accordingly US companies are characterized by short-term employment, frequent performance reviews, rapid promotion, specialized career paths, explicit control mechanisms, individual decision-making and responsibility, while Japanese companies are characterized by lifetime employment, rare performance reviews, slow promotion, meandering career paths, implicit control mechanisms and above all collective decision-making and responsibility. Type Z companies are hybrids that were originally American but have developed Japanese characteristics without actually copying Japanese companies. They are notable for the fact that their culture is defined by trust, friendship and cooperation. At the beginning of the 1980s Ouchi insisted that US companies should adopt his Theory Z in order to resist competition from Japan. Pascal and Athos (1981) recommend that more emphasis should be placed on the 'soft' variables of the management process than on the 'hard'. These are skills, staff, style and superordinate goals (ibid.; Peters and Waterman, 1982). When Western managers and scientists have tried to identify the Japanese methods that have brought success and how they could be used to benefit Western companies there has often been confusion between cause and effect. It is the qualifications of Japanese employees, their work ethos and their loyalty to the company that have allowed companies to develop the methods used to ensure competitiveness and long-term survival. Therefore it was not just individual management techniques and forms of work organization such as *kanban*, just-in-time or quality circles that have determined the success of Japanese companies.

Japanese human resource management is essential to understanding the competitiveness of Japanese companies. Underlying Japanese human resource management are a series of norms and principles that are maintained with great consistency in Japanese companies. Trust and loyalty between the company and the employees play as large a part as balancing management and staff interests to benefit the company. Indeed it would not be an exaggeration to say that the Japanese have a human resource philosophy that has overtones of employee equality. This philosophy is defined by intense communication between employees and their superiors that extends beyond the working day, a strong willingness on the part of employees to perform well, be disciplined and be committed to the company, and on the part of the company to care for its employees beyond the workplace relationship. Well-known characteristics of Japanese human resource management include particularly lifetime employment, seniority-based pay and promotion, and work councils oriented towards finding compromises between management and employees. Group orientation and harmony are essential preconditions for cooperation and bottom-up decision-making that involves all those who will be affected by the decision. These factors and patriarchal leadership have defined the character of Japanese human resource management, but does this still hold true today? What changes has Japanese human resource management undergone in recent years?

In the 1990s and at the beginning of the twenty-first century the Japanese economy was no longer able to maintain the dynamic growth of the previous decades and brief periods of economic recovery were followed by recessions. In Japan the 1990s are often called the 'lost decade'. During that period the environmental conditions changed dramatically for Japanese companies. While this should have prompted changes to human resource management, there was a strong tendency to retain the norms that had led to companies' earlier economic success. Nonetheless many companies recognized the necessity of restructuring their human resource practices in order to remain competitive. The seniority principle, which contributed to stability and loyalty and was central to lifetime employment, not only incurred high labour costs but could also have the effect of suppressing motivation and creativity among younger employees. It was at these two levels that most of the innovations in human resource management were initiated, although the associated measures were often introduced hesitantly and incompletely.

The chapters in this volume investigate continuity and innovation in Japanese human resource management from different points of view. The changing structure of the Japanese labour market is having a considerable impact on corporate policy. In Chapter 2 Tadashi Hanami looks at this topic and at industrial relations and labour policy. In Chapter 3 Hiromasa Suzuki describes the development of different forms of human resource management over the course of the twentieth century. During that time Japanese human resource management underwent significant changes in response to changes in the economy. Today Japanese companies are again searching for new solutions to meet the challenge of intensified global competition, and therefore the traditional human resource practices are being closely scrutinized.

In Chapter 4 Michio Nitta tackles the subject of employment adjustment since the financial crisis. He explains that despite the employment adjustments made by companies after the crisis, employment practices continued to function much as they had always done. Moreover the pace of employment adjustment, was significantly slower than it had been during the recessions that had followed the first oil crisis in the mid 1970s and the extreme appreciation of the yen that had accompanied the Plaza Accords in the mid 1980s. John Benson (Chapter 5) looks at emerging patterns of human resource management in Japan. He discusses how the global success of Japanese companies was supported by internal labour markets and stable relationships between all stakeholders. Age-based wages and promotion, lifetime employment and strong employee commitment allowed companies to increase their market share while reducing unit costs and improving quality. However the low economic growth during the 1990s and increasing global competition placed pressure on Japanese manufacturing companies to reconsider their human resource practices. Benson deliberates on whether the changes made have extended to the basic human resource management architecture, and in order to assess the durability of the human resource reforms he sets out to identify the key drivers of change.

Next Markus Pudelko (Chapter 6) looks at decision-making in Japanese companies. He outlines the strengths and weakness of the traditional decision-making process in Japanese companies and investigates how it has changed in recent years in response to changing circumstances. In Chapter 7 Jun Imai and Karen Shire discuss employment deregulation and the expanding market for temporary labour in Japan. Deregulation and the growth of the temporary employment sector have resulted in greater use of the external labour market as a source of skilled labour. In the late 1990s many companies reduced the size of their permanent workforce and made greater use of workers and external workers on fixed-term contracts.

Part-time work remained the largest form of non-regular employment, but resort to these two types of temporary employment grew rapidly between 1997 and 2002. While deregulation opened the way for temporary employment, temporary employment firms played a leading role in organizing the market for temporary employees and, branched out into a range of personnel services, including recruitment, training and the preretirement transfer of redundant older workers, functions that had traditionally been the realm of the human resource departments of Japanese firms.

In Chapter 8 David Methé and Junichiro Miyabe ask 'can *Mikoshi* management survive?', in Chapter 9 Hiroyuki Fujimura discusses the trend for employees to develop their own vocational skills, and in Chapter 10 Philippe Debroux addresses a subject of great importance to Japanese companies: the shift towards a performance-based human resource management system. Peter Berg, Eileen Appelbaum, Tom Bailey and Arne L. Kalleberg consider employees' control of their working time in Chapter 11. They compare the situations in the United States, Germany and Japan and conclude that while control over the duration and timing of work remains largely in managements' hands, employees in certain countries have gained some control over their working time. They also show that in Japan, where company unions are weak and employment regulations are not strictly enforced, employers tend to set the type and structure of working time, and little power or control is placed in the hands of employees.

Chapter 12 is a report from practical experience. In it Mahito Yamao and Markus Falk discuss the route taken in Japan by the German company BASF in respect of personnel policy. In the final chapter (Chapter 13) Frank Schulz addresses the subject of staff recruitment. Based on practical experience he describes and analyses recruitment in Japan and outlines successful strategies for and forms of recruitment.

It is hoped that this volume will be of help to academics and practitioners who are interested in the processes of change in Japanese human resource management, and that it will encourage both to engage in discussions of the associated problems.

References

Abegglen, J. C. (1958) *The Japanese Factory: Aspects of its Social Organization* (Glencoe, Ill.: The Free Press).

Abernathy, W., K. Clark and A. Kantrow (1981) 'The New Industrial Competition', *Harvard Business Review*, 59 (September–October), pp. 69–81.

Aoki, M. (1988) *Information, Incentives, and Bargaining in the Japanese Economy* (Cambridge: Cambridge University Press).

Aoki, M. (1989) 'The Nature of the Japanese Firm as a Nexus of Employment and Financial Contracts: An Overview', *Journal of Japanese International Economics*, 3, pp. 345–366.

Aoki, M. (1990) 'Towards an Economic Model of the Japanese Firm', *Journal of Economic Literature*, 38 (1), pp. 1–27.

Aoki, M. (1994) 'The Japanese Firm as a System of Attributes: A Survey and Research Agenda', in M. Aoki and R. Dore (eds), *The Japanese Firm. Source of Competitive Strength* (Oxford: Oxford University Press), pp. 11–40.

Aoki, M. (2000) *Information, Corporate Governance, and Institutional Diversity. Competitiveness in Japan, the USA, and the Transitional Economies* (Oxford: Oxford University Press).

Aoki, M. and R. Dore (eds) (1994) *The Japanese Firm. Source of Competitive Strength* (Oxford: Oxford University Press).

Ballon, R. J. (2002) 'Human Resource Management and Japan', *Euro Asia Journal of Management*, 12, pp. 5–20.

Chandler, A. (1990) *Scale and Scope. The Dynamics of Industrial Capitalism* (Cambridge, Mass.: Belknap Press).

Chandler, A. (1992) 'Managerial Enterprise and Competitive Capabilities', *Business History*, 34, pp. 11–41.

Cole, R. E. (1972) 'Permanent Employment in Japan: Fact and Fantasies', *Industrial and Labor Relations Review*, 26 (1), pp. 615–30.

Dore, R. (1973) *British Factory–Japanese Factory* (Berkeley, CA: University of California Press).

Hayes, R. and W. Abernathy (1980) 'Managing Our Way to Industrial Decline', *Harvard Business Review*, 58 (July–August), pp. 69–77.

Hazama, H. (1997) *The History of Labour Management in Japan* (London: Macmillan).

Hirakubo, N. (1999) 'The End of Lifetime Employment in Japan', *Business Horizon*, 42 (6), pp. 41–6.

Hofstede, G. (2001) *Culture's Consequences. Comparing Values, Behaviors, Institutions and Organizations across Nations*, 2nd edn (London and Thousand Oaks, CA: Sage).

Imai, K. (1989) 'Evolution of Japan's Corporate and Industrial Networks', in B. Carlsson (ed.), *Industrial Dynamics: Technological, Organizational, and Structural Changes in Industries and Firms* (Dordrecht: Springer), pp. 123–55.

Itagaki, H. (2004) 'Characteristics and Future of the Japanese Corporate Management System', paper presented at the Euro-Asia Management Studies Association Annual Conference, Hong Kong, 3–6 November.

Johnson, C. (1982) *MITI and the Japanese Miracle. The Growth of Industrial Policy 1925–1975* (Stanford, CA: Stanford University Press).

Kono, T. and S. Clegg (2001) *Trends in Japanese Management. Continuing Strengths, Current Problems and Changing Priorities* (Basingstoke and New York: Palgrave).

Koshiro, K. (2000) *A Fifty Year History of Industry and Labour in Postwar Japan* (Tokyo: Japan Institute of Labour).

Magota, R. (1970) *Nenko-Chingin no Ayumi to Mirai–Chingin Taikei 100 Nen-shi* (The Past and Future of the Seniority Wage System–100 years of the Japanese Wage System) (Tokyo: Sangyo J Chosa-sho).

Maslow, A. H. (1954) *Motivation and Personality* (New York: Harper & Row).

Matanle, P. (2003) *Japanese Capitalism and Modernity in a Global Era. Re-fabricating Lifetime Employment Relations* (London and New York: RoutledgeCurzon).

McGregor, D. (1960) *The Human Side of Enterprise* (New York: McGraw-Hill).

Morishima, M. (1995) 'The Japanese Human Resource Management System: A Learning Bureaucracy', in L. Moore and P. Jennings (eds), *Human Resource Management on the Pacific Rim. Institutions, Practices, and Attitudes* (Berlin and New York: Walter de Gruyter), pp. 119–50.

Nonaka, I. (1988) 'Towards Middle-Up Down Management: Accelerating Information Creation', *Sloan Management Review*, 29 (Spring), pp. 9–18.

Odagiri, H. (1992) *Growth through Competition, Competition through Growth. Strategic Management and the Economy in Japan* (Oxford: Oxford University Press).

Ouchi, W. (1981) *Theory Z: How American Business Can Meet the Japanese Challenge* (Reading, Mass.: Addison-Wesley).

Ouchi, W. G. and J. B. Johnson (1978) 'Types of Organizational Control and Their Relationship to Emotional Well Being', *Administrative Science Quarterly*, 23 (2), pp. 293–317.

Pascal, R. T. and A. G. Athos (1981) *The Art of Japanese Management* (Harmondsworth: Penguin).

Penrose, E. (1959) *The Theory of the Growth of the Firm* (Oxford: Oxford University Press).

Peters, T. J. and R. H. Waterman (1982) *In Search of Excellence* (New York: Harper & Row).

Porter, M. (1990) *The Competitive Advantage of Nations* (New York: Free Press).

Porter, M., H. Takeuchi and M. Sakakibara (2000) *Can Japan Compete?* (London: Macmillan).

Sugimoto, Y. (2003) *An Introduction to Japanese Society*, 2nd edn (Cambridge: Cambridge University Press).

Sullivan, J. J. (1992) 'Japanese Management Philosophies: From the Vacuous to the Brilliant', *California Management Review*, 34 (2), pp. 66–87.

Suzuki, Y. (1991) *Japanese Management Structures, 1920–1980* (Basingstoke: Macmillian).

Sydow, J. (1992) *Strategische Netzwerke – Evolution und Organisation* (Wiesbaden: Gabler).

Woronoff, J. (1992) *The Japanese Management Mystique. The Reality Behind the Myth* (Chicago, Ill., and Cambridge: Irwin).

Yanashita, K. (2001) *Wakariyasui Jinji ga Kaisha o Kaeru* (Simple HRM Can Change a Company) (Tokyo: Nihon Keizai Shimbunsha).

2
The Changing Labour Market, Industrial Relations and Labour Policy[1]

Tadashi Hanami

The pros and cons of the Japanese model

The merits of Japanese-style management have recently been disputed as the Japanese economy continues to suffer from persistent difficulties. After the collapse of the bubble economy the once world-acclaimed Japanese model came to be regarded by many as inefficient and incompatible with reform. More recently the system has been re-evaluated, and business leaders have successfully revamped their companies amidst the persistent stagnation of Japanese business.

Fujio Mitarai – the president of Canon, which is doing remarkably well internationally in the field of information technology – highlights the value of corporate loyalty to the expansion of Japanese activities in the global market. However he warns that although corporate loyalty flourishes under the traditional lifetime employment system it can result in inertia among employees if they consider that their jobs will always be protected by the system. To avoid this he believes that companies should reward those who achieve results through their own ingenuity (Mitarai, 2003). The economist Yukio Suzuki (2003) notes that the main problem faced by Japanese companies today is how to link performance evaluation to employee motivation. Japanese employees are known throughout the world for their diligence, loyalty, intelligence and teamwork. The question is how best to make use of these qualities. Suzuki concludes that ultimately it boils down to leadership by top management and employees' trust in management.

A typical example of this is the revival of Nissan Motors. As president and CEO, over the past five years. Carlos Ghosn has dramatically revitalized the once seriously troubled company. He expresses his high regard for the 'three valuable characteristics [of the Japanese management model]: seniority wages, lifetime employment and (relative) concentration of power in middle-class management' (Ghosn, 2003, p. 138). In his opinion Nissan's troubles were due not to Japanese-style management but to the company being constrained by old customs and failing to adjust. He emphasizes that competitive Japanese companies have secured high profits by retaining the strengths of the Japanese system while adopting features of international management in their global operations. The companies that have proved successful are those which have added performance evaluation to the lifetime employment system, but only competitive companies with large profits can adhere to the later. Thus he concludes that 'lifetime employment is a target, not a rule' (ibid.).

Are lifetime employment and revitalization of the Japanese economy compatible?

Media attention recently focused on two cases where enterprises that were thought to be impossible to revive had made spectacular recoveries: Nissan Motors and the Hanshin Tigers, a professional baseball team. Nissan, once one of the most successful of the automotive giants, suffered a serious business decline in 1999. The number of cars sold dropped to about half that sold by Toyota, plants were running at little more than 50 per cent of their capacity and the company's accumulated deficit amounted to 2 trillion yen. In the spring of 1999 Carlos Ghosn from Renault took over as CEO. Under his leadership the company recorded a profit increase of 4.75 per cent in 2000, 7.9 per cent in 2001 and 10.5 per cent in the first half of 2002. In 2004 it was expecting to increase its sales by one million cars.

Meanwhile the Hanshin Tigers had been struggling to win a game and always ended the season towards the bottom of the league, if not at the very bottom. Senichi Hoshino, a successful former manager of the Chunichi Dragons, was appointed skipper in 2002. Under his leadership the team was dramatically revitalized and captured the pennant in 2003, 18 years after its last championship win in 1985. The team had attracted 3.3 million fans to its games that season and it is estimated to have generated spending of several hundred million dollars in the Kansai area (home of the team), including sales of Hanshin-brand goods and spending on food and drink.

On 17 September 2003 the *Nikkei*, the Japanese equivalent of the *Wall Street Journal*, published a long article on Ghosn's Nissan and Hoshino's Hanshin Tigers, praising them as 'the new business models that will lead to a rebirth of enterprises'. The two cases had five common features:

- Both leaders came from the outside and made drastic changes.
- They implanted a spirit of competition: Ghosn introduced a pay system based on results and Hoshino made players compete against each other for field positions.
- Both made personnel changes: Ghosn recruited employees from Toyota and Honda and transferred workers to other departments, while Hoshino hired coaching staff and players from other teams.
- They engaged in bold restructuring: Ghosn closed five factories in Japan and laid off 20,000 workers, including overseas facilities, and Hoshino replaced one third of the players by outsiders.
- Both leaders were notable for their effort to communicate: Ghosn placed great emphasis on dialogue with employees and Hoshino praised players for their positive contributions.

All five features appear to be incompatible with Japanese-style management and traditional employment practices. However the first, third and fourth reflected the overall flexibilization of the labour market, and the second and fifth, were more or less in line with the traditional notions of teamwork and individual initiative. Nonetheless bringing in top leaders from the outside contradicted the traditional principle of promotion from within, and recruiting personnel from other companies, particularly to fill high-ranking managerial and professional positions, was a very unusual step, as was laying off workers, which hitherto had been regarded as the very last resort for enterprises faced with economic difficulties.[2]

These two cases of innovative revival can be viewed as an indication of the future of the traditional Japanese management system. It is obvious that the system cannot survive unless some of its basic premises are revised or rejected. In this regard developments at major companies such as Hitachi, Canon and others point to abandonment of seniority-based wage system and its replacement by performance-related pay. Hitachi is unique in extending its performance-evaluation system for higher-ranking employees to its 30,000 regular employees. Under the new system an employee's wages are not increased and even may be reduced if the performance evaluation is sufficiently negative (*Nikkei Shinbun*, 5 November 2003). This is noteworthy in that although many companies introduced performance-related pay several decades ago they have not entirely abolished the traditional seniority-based wage system. It has been reported that other leading companies – including Toyota,

Mitsubishi, Chubu Electric Power and Takeda Chemicals – are following suit (*Asahi Shinbun*, 6 November 2003).

Lifetime employment and the reality of the labour market

Regardless of the merits of lifetime employment, the practice is declining in terms of the number of workers covered by the system and the role it plays in the Japanese labour market.

According to labour force surveys the number of employees with fixed-term contracts rose from around 910,000 in 1992 to more than two million in 2001. Moreover in 2001 there were 12 million part-time workers (working fewer than 35 hours per week), representing an increase in part-time workers' share of the total workforce from 10 per cent in 1980 to 22.8 per cent in 2001. For male part-time workers the rise was from 5.2 per cent to 12 per cent and for females it was from 19.3 per cent to 39.1 per cent (Ministry of Public Management, Home Affairs, Post and Telecommunications, 2002). A large majority of part-time workers are middle-aged married women,[3] followed by elderly and young male workers.

The number of temporary workers hired from agencies (called 'dispatched workers' in Japan) nearly tripled from 503,000 in 1992 to around 1.45 million in 2001 (Japan Institute of Labour, 2003). This means that in 2001 the number of non-regular employees reached 13.8 million, or 26 per cent of the total workforce excluding executives, while the number of regular employees had dropped by 2.1 million since 1992 (10.4 million males and 10.5 million females). Thus non-regular employees accounted for about a third the total number of employed people (Ministry of Public Management, Home Affairs, Post and Telecommunications, 2002).

On 28 October, 2003 the *Nikkei* reported a survey on the future employment strategies of the top 1000 companies. According to the survey, on average Japanese companies planned to reduce their intake of new graduates by 7 per cent while increasing the intake of other outsiders by 9.3 per cent. The figures were highest for the electronics industry, where the intake of outsiders would rise by 24.1 per cent and that of graduates would be reduced by 12.1 per cent. This reflects the general changes that are being made to employment practices in Japan.

Thus the labour market situation suggests that in spite of the merits of lifetime employment, both the scope of its coverage and its role are declining and policy makers have to face up to this reality.

Negative legacies of lifetime employment

Lifetime employment has two serious consequences. First, it has created a discriminatory employment structure. Traditionally the privileges associated with lifetime employment, such as guaranteed job security and better working conditions, have only been available to males recruited directly from school or university. Women, minority groups, foreigners and those who have failed in education or in their first job have been excluded from such privileges. Non-regular workers have always been used as shock absorbers during business fluctuations but otherwise sacrificed for the job security of regular workers.

Because of the inadequate antidiscrimination laws[4] women workers are concentrated in part-time employment. In addition women, together with minority groups and foreigners (especially undocumented ones) dominate other types of non-regular employment, including temporary and agency work. Such work has little job security, lower wages and none of the fringe benefits enjoyed by regular workers. The wage gap between full-time and part-time workers has grown in recent years. Between 1989 and 2001 the hourly income of female part-time workers dropped from 70.9 per cent to 66.4 per cent of that of female full-time workers; for men the drop was from 55.7 per cent to 50.7 per cent (Ministry of Health, Labour and Welfare, 2002).

Second, lifetime employment has weakened trade unionism and worker protection. The individual enterprise unions have tended to cater only to regular employees covered by lifetime employment, mostly in larger enterprises. Due to a declining unionization rate they have recently tried to organize non-regular workers, but mostly in vain. It is reported that less than 3 per cent of the more than 10 million part-time workers are organized (Ministry of Health, Labor and Welfare 2002). In one major supermarket chain, where part-timers account for more than 80 per cent of the workforce, only 1 per cent of workers are organized.

Because of the serious drop in the unionization rate (from 28.9 per cent in 1985 to 20.7 per cent in 2001) and the declining influence of trade unions in general, Rengo (the country's top labour federation) set up a committee of outside experts to evaluate its activities and make recommendations. The committee's report, published in September 2002, was blunt in its condemnations. It noted that the organization's leaders had lost touch with rank-and-file members, and commented on the series of scandals that had rocked some unions, including the All Japan Municipal Workers' Union, one of the most powerful unions affiliated with Rengo. The report said that Rengo seemed only to be concerned with the interests of privileged male workers at large corporations and was neglecting disadvantaged workers who badly need help, including those suffering from poor working conditions, part-time and temporary workers, and workers in small companies with fewer than 100 employees.

Despite the findings of the committee, at the Rengo's annual convention in autumn 2003 Kiyoshi Sasamori was re-elected chairman, beating Tsuyoshi Takagi, leader of the Japanese Federation of Textile, Garment, Chemical, Mercantile, Food and Allied Workers Union. According to a *Japan Times* columnist, 'Takagi should have been elected its leader. Sasamori's re-election shows that Rengo's member unions have become complacent about the leadership of big-company unions' (Hanai, 2003, p. 14). Hanai also pointed out that Rengo was neglecting the interests of women, who should be encouraged to take part in union activities.

Inadequate labour policies

In June 2003 an amendment was made to the Labour Standards Law requiring just cause to dismiss workers. Under previous case law companies could only be taken to court for abuse of the right to dismiss. Although it is generally agreed that this amendment has given greater protection to workers, in practice it may adversely affect those who are seeking employment. For example it could make employers reluctant to hire workers for permanent jobs, and instead hire only part-time or temporary workers for non-permanent jobs. Thus in the event of an economic downturn they would be able to cut jobs without facing charges of unfair dismissal.

For several decades the government has been encouraging employers to re-evaluate the company retirement age. In 1994 legislation was passed that set the compulsory retirement age at 60, but soon after the implementation of the 2003 Labour Standards Law provision on the right to dismiss, the Minister of Welfare, Labour and Health expressed his intention to raise the retirement age to 65 (*Nikkei*, 15 October 2003). Apparently the government is taking steps to afford greater protection to older workers.

Another amendment introduced in 2003 extended the maximum period of short-term employment contracts, changed the rules on the use of dispatch workers, and relaxed the regulations on the flexible working hour system.[5] There had been an attempt to make most of these changes in 1998 but the attempt had been abandoned due to strong union opposition. The unions' main argument that had been allowing longer periods of short-term employment would negatively affect regular employees.

The above was another example of union leaders being so concerned with the interests of privileged workers that they have paid no heed to those badly in need of any kind of job, be it for a long or short period. They do not understand the rather simple premise that strict regulations on periods of employment and restrictions on flexible working systems can damage the spirit of entrepreneurship, and therefore restrict business growth.

As long as unions only represent the interests of secure workers and male employees at larger corporations and can remain complacent about union–management relations, as Hanai (2003) has pointed out it is only natural that they will continue to defend policies that protect those workers and ignore the interests of underprivileged non-members. Under the present administrative system, decision-making on labour policy, is undertaken by trilateral committees established by the Ministry of Health, Labour and Welfare. These committees consist of representatives of labour, representatives of employers and neutral outsiders with knowledge and experience. The labour and employer representatives are appointed by the ministry based on recommendations by the most representative organizations on each side. In the case of labour, this is usually Rengo or its affiliated unions. The result is a cosy and complacent relationship among the committee members and resistance to any measure that would change the *status quo*, including legislation on discrimination. Rather than an abstract prohibition or dismissal without just cause, what is required is legislation to prevent discrimination in hiring, job assignment and promotion based on race, nationality or family origin, sex, age, disability and so on. The present author has tried in vain to gain support for such legislation inside and outside the committees.

Of course antidiscrimination legislation could reduce job opportunities for disadvantaged groups if it were introduced without careful consideration of the possible effects. But at the same time the Japanese soft approach to law enforcement, which relies on administrative guidance rather than direct enforcement through a court order or penalty, is not very effective, as evidenced by the government's miserable efforts to enforce the Equal Employment Opportunity Law since its introduction in 1985 (Hanami, 1998) and to improve the working conditions of part-time workers. As already mentioned, the wage gap between part-timers and regular workers has expanded rather than narrowed. Thus unions must broaden their focus or be replaced by bodies that are willing to fight for the policies so desperately needed by the disadvantaged groups whose interests have been ignored for so long.

Notes

1. This chapter was originally published in *Japan Labor Review*, 1 (1) (2004).
2. Reduction of the workforce to improve corporate finances or avoid bankruptcy can still be regarded as violations of the legal principle of abuse of the right to dismiss, and is therefore illegal under Japanese case law.
3. The proportion of women in part-time employment has consistently been around 70 per cent since 1990 (OECD, 2002).
4. For the inadequacy of the antidiscrimination laws in Japan, and particularly the Equal Employment Opportunity Act, see Hanami (1998–2000).
5. The maximum period for employment contracts was extended from one to three years, and from three to five years for professional jobs and people older than 60. The discretionary system for work at headquarters was extended to include work outside the headquarters. The maximum period for the employment of dispatched workers was extended from one to three years, and the types of job that dispatched workers could be employed for were extended to include jobs in the manufacturing sector (previously prohibited). Moreover the three-year maximum period for employing dispatched workers for 24 designated professional jobs was abolished, and employers were obliged to continue to employ dispatched workers if the latter wished to stay when the dispatching period was over.

References

Ghosn, C. (2003) 'Waga nihonteki keiei no sinzui wo kataro' (Talking about the gist of my Japanese-style management), *Bungei Shunju*, August, pp. 138–46.
Hanai, K. (2003) 'Resuscitating Japanese Labor', *Japan Times*, 27 October.
Hanami, T. (1998) 'Equal Employment Opportunity in Japan – the Crossroads of Japanese Corporate and Legal Culture', in C. Engels and M. Weiss (eds), *Labour Law and Industrial Relations at the Turn of the Century* (The Hague: Kluwer).
Hanami, T. (2000) 'Equal Employment Revisited', *Japan Labour Bulletin*, 39 (1), pp. 5–10.
Japan Institute of Labour (2003) *Japanese Working Life Profile* (Tokyo: Japan Institute of Labour), p. 41.
Ministry of Health, Labour and Welfare (2002) *Final Report of Study Committee on Part-time Work* (Tokyo: Ministry of Health, Labour and Welfare).
Ministry of Public Management, Home Affairs, Post and Telecommunications (2002) *Report on the Labour Force Survey* (Tokyo: Ministry of Public Management, Home Affairs, Posts and Telecommunications).
Mitarai, F. (2003) 'Aikokusin naki keizaikaikaku wa sippaisuru' (Reform without patriotism will fail), *Bungei Shunju*, July.
OECD (2002) *Labor Force Statistics* (Paris: OECD).
Suzuki, Y. (2003) 'Japanese-style management deserves updated appraisal', *Japan Times*, 21 July.
Yashiro, N. (1999) *Koyoh Kaikaku no Zidai* (Era of employment reform) (Tokyo: Chuoh Kohron).

3
The Changing Models of Human Resource Management in Japanese Firms: A Long-Term View

Hiromasa Suzuki

Introduction

Past discussions of Japanese human resource management (HRM) have revolved around the so-called Japanese employment system, in which permanent employees (nearly always male) of large firms enjoy lifetime employment and good promotion prospects. These firms, which are completely segregated from the external labour market, recruit employees directly from high school or university and provide on-the-job training, often combined with regular job rotation. The investment in training is worthwhile because the employees are there for the long term. In order to avoid the inefficiencies and rigidities associated with lifetime employment, firms encourage fierce competition among employees but treat them in an egalitarian way (small wage differentials, more or less equal promotion up to the age of 35 or so).

This employment system is regarded as the core of the Japanese management system. However since the bubble economy burst in 1991, a long and continuous recession has rendered the system inappropriate and most firms are seeking flexibility by introducing other forms of employment and outsourcing.

This chapter looks at the evolution of Japanese HRM over time. It identifies three HRM models. The first emerged in the 1920s and 1930s in some large firms and was based on the division between blue-collar workers and a limited number of white-collar or technical employees. After World War II, dramatic changes took place in some social and economic institutions (education, industrial relations, production) and firms had to adapt to these changes. The lifetime employment model was shaped and perfected in the 1960s and 1970s, when economic growth was high. The long recession in the 1990s exerted strong pressure on this model and HRM became much more stratified, with a limited number of core workers and considerable use of atypical workers. From a certain point of view, this could be seen as going back to square one.

The chapter is structured in the following way. In the following section the three basic HRM models will be discussed. The subsequent section examines the models' underlying ideology, and the final section considers recent transformations of HRM.

The three models of Japanese HRM

HRM is a tool whose functioning depends on corporate culture, technological requirements or broader societal factors. Some firms emphasize short-term management functions, with adequate staffing and control of labour costs being the principal preoccupation of HRM directors. In other firms HRM has a strategic function and the aim is the long-term development of human resources. In research-oriented firms (for instance those in the pharmaceutical or IT industries) the recruitment and development of high-calibre employees is a constant preoccupation. In any given period different types of HRM may coexist, depending on the specificity of the firm or its corporate culture. However there is usually a dominant model that is tailored to the prevailing economic situation. The following subsections consider the three successive models that emerged in the twentieth century.

HRM in the prewar, interwar and postwar years

There have been numerous studies of the history of HRM during the industrialization of Japan (see for example Hirschmeier and Yui 1975, 1977; Hazma, 1978; Shirai, 1992). Prior to World War I, industrial development was limited to the textile industries (cotton and silk) and some light consumer products. Heavy industries were either in the public sector or heavily subsidized by the state. In this period managers had little need to be preoccupied with human resources since firms relied on labour bosses to assemble the required number of workers on a contractual basis. This was similar to the situation in the United States before the scientific management era.

World War I was a boom period for the nascent Japanese industries because exports from Europe were frozen and there was a huge demand for Japanese products. Modern industries took off at this period, in part due to the development of the *zaibatsu* (Mitsui, Mitsubishi and Sumitomo). After the war there was a series of recessions and managers had to take tighter control of their organizations. Also, investment in capital equipment and the consequent need for industrial skills rather than craft skills made it necessary to shift from indirect to direct management of human resources. During this period the recruitment of university graduates for engineering and management jobs was systematized so as to provide future core staff. The HRM model was incrementally shaped by the large *zaibatsu* firms and then gradually extended to other firms.

In this HRM model there were three categories of workers: top managers, management staff and professionals (*shoku-in*) and operatives (*ko-in*). Each of the three groups was kept separate from the others, and particularly the *shoku-in* from the *ko-in*. Management staff and professionals were recruited from universities and paid on a monthly basis. Additional benefits such as bonuses, housing and retirement pensions were provided. Employment was long term, although no formal contracts were signed. In all likelihood the number of managers and professionals was small, and they constituted an elite class with a stable career and protected employment. Operatives were generally recruited from junior high school and were paid on a daily basis. Employment was normally stable but without formal protection. Top managers were a class apart. In leading *zaibatsu*, top executives such as Takashi Masuda and Takuma Dan made all the appointments to senior management posts.[1] Pay differentials between categories were as important as individual differentiation. Indeed HRM was entirely based on hierarchy, with a handful of well-paid white-collar staff managing blue-collar workers.

Unions were formed after the end of World War I (influenced by the establishment of the ILO), but their impact was limited. They were organized by trade or occupation rather than at the enterprise level, as was the case in the later period. Labour–management committees were often set up at the factory level to avoid union influence.

HRM in the high-growth period (1960–75)

The second model – in which lifetime employment, seniority-based pay and enterprise unionism formed the main pillars (Magota, 1970; Shirai, 1992) – is so well known that a detailed description is not required here. Hence we shall merely highlight the differences between it and the previous one.

Firstly, the second model applied to all permanent employees of a firm and there was no distinction between blue-collar and white-collar workers. Egalitarian treatment, or at least in principle, was its most notable feature. This was mainly a consequence of the social reforms introduced by General MacArthur in his capacity as supreme commander of the Allied powers. One of the first demands made by the newly created union movement had been the abolition of status differentials such as blue and white collar. However the war-time wage policy had already prepared the ground for the harmonization of status, the provision of health insurance, fixed allowances for all workers and the narrowing of wage differentials (Magota, 1970).

Secondly, the model was perfectly suited to the growth of companies and the economy. The seniority-based pay system was conducive to cost saving in that the abundant supply of young labour meant that growing firms could recruit a large number of young workers with low starting wages. If the firms could keep the average age of employees low the work force would cost less than its marginal product. By the same token, continuous growth was necessary to ensure internal career prospects, since growing firms could create more managerial or professional posts. As a result of extensive on-the-job training and work experience, senior workers were more skilled than young workers – a necessary precondition for the seniority-based wage system. These conditions were perfectly met in the leading industries (electrical machinery, ship building, the steel industry and so on).

Thirdly, the personnel department was in a strong position and often reported directly to the CEO. Recruitment, job assignment, on-the-job training, job rotation and internal promotion were often centralized and coordinated by the department. Moreover the chief of personnel was involved in most important decisions, including the appointment of top managerial staff.

Flexible HRM

From the beginning of the 1990s, radical changes took place in the economic climate and a series of recessions meant that most firms had to adjust to stagnating or diminishing demand. With real incomes falling, consumers became much more sensitive to price and product quality, and firms were faced by less stable and predictable domestic markets. In addition deregulation hit firms and organizations (financial organizations, telecommunication companies, public corporations) that had previously been protected, by exposing them to competitive pressure.

Most firms were forced to reduce the number of lifetime workers. This was achieved by recruiting fewer graduates, restructuring certain activities and introducing early retirement. Increases in the demand for workers were met by part-time workers, temporary workers or outsourcing.[2] The latter was largely used by manufacturing firms and sometimes entire production operations were outsourced to specialized companies, especially in the electronics and automotive industries. In the retail sector a considerable proportion of permanent employees were replaced by part-time workers or employees on fixed-term contracts that offered only limited employment protection.

In the course of all this, personnel departments lost a number of their functions. Because of financial constraints many firms could no longer afford to provide extensive on-the-job training and engage in regular job rotation, which previously had been handled by the personnel department. Moreover many large firms decentralized decision-making on recruitment, job assignment and internal promotion to their product divisions. Furthermore decisions on outsourcing and the recruitment of part-time and temporary workers were sometimes taken at the plant level or by project managers.

As a result of these developments today's HRM has in some respects returned to the past in that different categories of worker coexist in the same firm, there is no long-term perspective on human resource development and performance targets tend to be short term.

The underlying ideology of the HRM models

Although HRM models are management tools designed to suit the prevailing economic and social conditions, they always have an ideological basis. The pre- and interwar model was associated with paternalism and the family. One of the most popular managers of that period was S. Mutou of the textile firm Kanebo. In 1920 he referred to paternalism in a speech to law school graduates at the University of Tokyo:

> The Japanese family system differs from the Western one in that there is a warm spirit of mutual respect and sacrifice, each member contributing according to his ability ... I claim that paternalism is necessary for labour matters because the paternal generosity that exists in a family is most useful in the relationship between employer and employees. (Quoted in Hirschmeier and Yui, 1977, p. 321)

Mutou was a leading member of the Mitsui group, and as such can be considered a spokesman for Japanese industry. Another example was

S. Goto, who presided over the newly merged national railways and repeatedly spoke of the need for trust and love at work. His main theme was that corporations should be operated as an extended family, with trust and love serving as a moral guide.

One might question whether such paternalism was a more formality or had a real social foundation. In this respect it is important to note that Mutou and Goto were not capitalists; they were university-educated professional managers. At that time there was no real mobility between top management, white-collar and blue-collar jobs and segregation was the norm. The paternalistic approach appears to have been a play to diminish the influence of the increasingly radical unions during the economic downturn in the 1920s.

The model that emerged during the high-growth period after World War II had a totally different ideological basis. Thanks to the postwar reforms, elite managers nominated by the *zaibatsu* owners disappeared completely, and so did the social division between white-collar and blue-collar workers. The top managers came from the ranks of senior employees after a lengthy internal competition. They tended to value egalitarian treatment (the same starting wage for everybody) and long-term attachment. The three pillars of the management system – lifetime employment, seniority-based pay and enterprise unions – were regarded as part of the social contract between the firm and its employees. Managers and employees were viewed as being in the same boat and the prosperity of the firm would ensure a bright future for all. The only similarity between this model and the previous one was that firms tried hard to subdue radical labour activists. They did so by means of closed-shop union agreements (one union per firm). There was no need to resort to ideological discourses because all permanent employees saw themselves as sharing the fruits of economic growth.

Two well-known researchers have closely studied the mechanisms of HRM during this period. Koike is a prolific writer on Japanese firms and has conducted field studies in work places in Japan and overseas for more than four decades.[3] He coined the expression 'the white collariza-tion of Japanese blue-collar workers'; that is, the way in which blue-collar workers came to be treated exactly the same as white-collar workers (in terms of training, wages and internal promotion). He highlights the versatile skills that Japanese workers acquire through on-the-job train-ing and shows that regular job rotation in similar work is essential to skill development. As in the West, career paths are based on specializa-tion (accounting, production management, sales and so on), but unlike in the West the promotion process is slow.

Nonaka is well known for his original work on knowledge-creating companies (Nonaka and Takeuchi, 1995). His focus is less on HRM than on the process by which organizational knowledge develops and innovation takes place in Japanese firms. He is a man of vision and insight. He discusses the way that Japanese firms create innovative new products. The original idea for a new product comes from individual engineers or managers, then the product is developed through trial and error by teamwork. If a technical breakthrough is achieved, then the organizational unit pours in the resources required to commercialize the new product. Nonaka remarks that the knowledge accumulated during the development process should be shared by the organization so that the next generation of products can start at a higher level. He uses empirical cases (the development of home bread-making machines, copy machines and so on) to illustrate the various processes involved in innovation.

Thus knowledge creation seems to rely on teamwork, long-term commitment and organizational learning, so the weakening of the model that prevailed during the high-growth period is threatening knowledge creation in Japanese firms.

The present HRM model is based on flexible labour, a strategy recommended *inter alia* by the OECD and employers' organizations, including Nikkeiren (the Japanese Federation of Employers' Organizations – see Nikkeiren, 1995). The main idea is that firms should have three pools of employees. The first pool would consist of core employees with long-term tenure and guaranteed career prospects, as in the former model. The second pool would comprise staff professionals whose career would be restricted to their own special field, implying that they would have limited access to managerial posts and a lower degree of employment protection. The third pool would consist of highly mobile, flexible employees.

There is nothing new in this concept, but the fact that the main employers' organization has recommended it has had a certain impact. Until Nikkeiren's recommendation large firms had not dared to restructure their work force for fear that this would trigger a downward movement of their share prices and damage their social reputation. But since the mid 1990s restructuring has become normal, even in long-established firms, and some firms have ceased to recruit permanent employees and instead use outsourcing and part-time and temporary workers. Today the idea of short-term flexibility is widely accepted by employers, and by some enterprise unions.

Transformation of HRM in the 1990s and beyond

Since the 1990s many Japanese firms have been struggling to survive and accordingly have made profound changes to their organization, particularly in regard to HRM.

As in other industrialized countries, one of the most conspicuous changes is the rise in atypical forms of employment. As discussed above, this means that the proportion of lifetime employees is diminishing (Figure 3.1).

In 1986 non-permanent employees accounted for about 17 per cent of the total Japanese workforce (excluding agriculture), but by 2002 the figure had risen to 23 per cent. In 2002, of the 14.5 million non-permanent employees, 11.4 per cent were part-time workers, 5.3 per cent were casual workers, 3.6 per cent were on short fixed-term contracts and 0.7 per cent were temporary agency workers. Two thirds of these workers

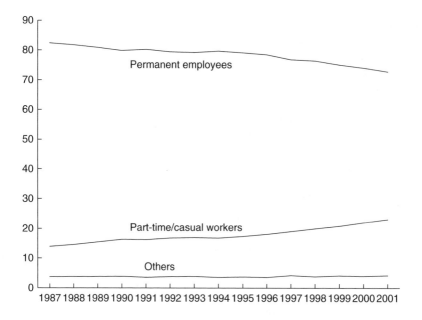

Source: Ministry of Health, Labour and Welfare (2003).

Figure 3.1   Employment trends, Japan, 1987–2001 (per cent)

were women. According to survey evidence, just over half of all female workers were employed on a non-permanent basis in 2002.

This overall increase of atypical employment is strongly related to the growth of the service sector, where the use of part-time and temporary workers is common. For example Nakata and Miyamoto (2002) have found that in the second half of the 1990s supermarkets and department stores were replacing permanent employees with such workers because the latter cost less in terms of wages and fringe benefits. However Ishihara (2003) has found that establishments that have reduced the number of full-time workers have not on the whole increased the number of part-time workers. This suggests that the growth of part-time jobs is attributable to job creation in particular sectors (transport and communications, services, finance and insurance) rather than to the replacement of full-time positions by part-time jobs.

In the case of outsourcing and the use of agency workers, gauging the extent of this requires panel data at the firm or plant level and such data is scarce. However we can estimate the extent of the restructuring efforts made by large firms quoted on the Tokyo Stock Market that report their number of permanent employees as well as financial information. Figure 3.2 shows three large electrical/electronics firms' total sales, operating profits and number of employees in the period 1990–2002. Two of the firms (designated here as A and B) were badly hit by the recession of 1997–98 and had to resort to serious restructuring. The measures included an almost total freeze on new recruitment, the separation of some activities from the main body of the company, relocation and outsourcing.

For instance Firm A, reduced its number of permanent employees by 37 per cent between 1998 and 2002, although the reduction was less at the group level (16.3 per cent). In contrast Firm C was able to weather the recession with little damage to sales or the workforce, thanks to the success of several new products. Today these firms extensively utilize outsourcing and agency workers to cope with volatile market conditions, and the relocation of production sites has been accelerated in recent years.

Finally, the measures taken by a large firm that makes precision machinery will be used here to illustrate how some firms modified their HRM in the 1990s. This firm, which has a high global ranking in its field, specializes in the production of parts for cars and machinery. It started overseas production as early as the 1970s in the United States and the United Kingdom, and more recently in Poland and China.

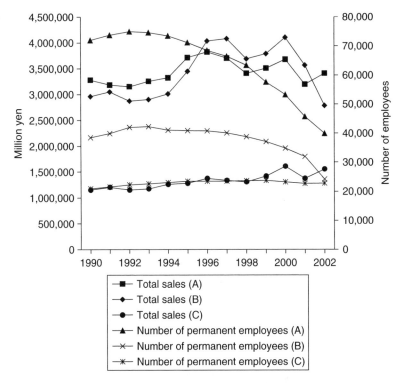

Figure 3.2 Total sales and number of permanent employees in three large electrical firms (A, B, C), 1990–2002

It also has several plants in Japan, which are managed as independent units specializing in particular products.

Plant A is an old factory producing parts for cars and plant B is a newer factory specializing in more varied and higher added-value products. Figures 3.3 and 3.4 show their sales and number of employees in 1990–2003.

Despite their different areas of specialization, the means of reducing employee numbers at these two plants were similar. The need for higher productivity was the primary motive for this reduction. There were no large redundancies, but posts that became vacant were filled by subcontractors, rather than new recruits. Subcontractors is now widely practised by manufacturing firms (the employment of temporary agency workers in manufacturing firms was forbidden by law until 2004).

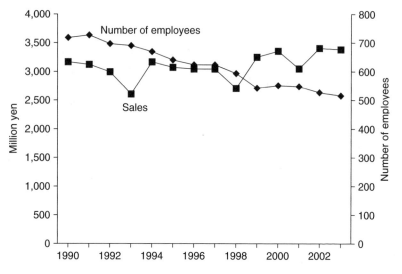

Figure 3.3   Sales and number of employees, plant A, 1990–2003

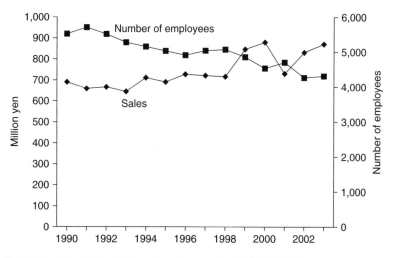

Figure 3.4   Sales and number of employees, plant B, 1990–2003

Indeed even routine surveillance work was entrusted to employees of subcontracting firms. All the firm's plants in Japan and abroad were given strict productivity and quality targets, with frequent reference to statistical targets.

The plants were in direct competition with similar plants in the United States, Poland and China, and reducing labour costs by outsourcing was one way of meeting this challenge. In the fierce drive to cut costs there was little room for the lifetime employment of the past. Atypical employment and outsourcing served the same purpose: the competitive pressures were so strong that each plant had to maximize output in the short term, leaving the coordinating function to the HR department.

Conclusions

The functioning of Japanese firms has changed drastically since the beginning of the 1990s due to recessions and competitive pressure in the global market. The nature of HRM has changed rapidly and atypical employment has become a notable feature. This chapter has examined the evaluation of Japanese HRM and its ideology and come to the following conclusions.

The HRM model that emerged during the interwar period was characterized by paternalism and segregation according to workplace status (management, white collar and blue collar). With the economic boom that began in 1960 this gave way to egalitarianism and lifetime employment. During this period the human resource department played a vital part in the management of the firm and handled all aspects of employment, including recruitment, on-the-job training, job rotation and promotion. However the economic crisis in the 1990s threw lifetime employment into question as many firms could not afford to continue to invest in training or guarantee jobs for life. The ongoing recession and market volatility demanded a much more flexible approach to HRM and product divisions were given considerable autonomy over employment matters. This was accompanied by changes to the wage system (particularly performance-related pay) and retirement allowances, as well as atypical forms of employment. The latter included greater use of part-time and temporary workers, outsourcing and subcontracting.

It is too soon to predict where these changes will lead, but it seems that the direction of change is not towards a new HRM model, but rather a return to the old interwar model.

Notes

1. Matsuda and Dan were the *de facto* managing directors of the entire Mitsui group. Both had an engineering background and had spent time in the United States in their youth. In contrast Mitsubishi was always managed by the founding family, Iwasaki.
2. The practice of outsourcing has been little studied, but it is estimated that tens of thousands of workers are engaged in fulfilling outsourced contracts. See Nakao (2004).
3. His various works are summarized in Koike (1996).

References

Hazama, H. (1978) *Nihon Romukanrishi Kenkyu* (Study of the history of HRM) (Tokyo: Ochanomizu Shobo).

Hirschmeier, J. and T. Yui (1975) *The Development of Japanese Business, 1600–1973* (Cambridge, Mass.: Harvard University Press).

Hirschmeier, J. and T. Yui (1977) *Nihon no Keieihatten* (Tokyo: Toyo Keizai Simposha).

Ishihara, M. (2003) 'Does Expansion of the Part-time Workforce Cause Contraction in the Full-time Workforce?', *Nihon Rodo Kenkyu Zasshi*, 45 (September), pp. 4–16.

Koike, K. (1996) *Shigotono Keizaigaku* (Economics of jobs) (Tokyo: Toyo Keizai Shimposha).

Magota, R. (1970) *Nenko chinging no Shuen* (The end of the seniority wage system) (Tokyo: Nikkei Shimbun).

Ministry of Health, Labour and Welfare (2003), *Kosei Rodo Hakusho* (White Paper on Labour) (Tokyo: Ministry of Health, Labour and Welfare).

Nakao, K. (2004) 'Denki Sangyo ni okeru Ukeoi Rodosha no Katsuyo to Ukeoi Tekiseika no Kadai' (Use of subcontractors in electrical industries and their problems of protection), *Nihon Rodo Kenkyu Zasshi* (*The Japanese Journal of Labour Studies*), May.

Nakata, Y. and D. Miyamoto (2002) 'Seiki Jugyoin no Koyou Sakugen to Hiseiki Rodou no Zoka' (Reduction of regular permanent employees and the rise of atypical work), in Y. Genda and Y. Nakata (eds), *Risutora to Tenshoku no Mecanisumu* (Mechanism of Restructuring and Labour Mobility) (Tokyo: Toyo Keizai Shinposha).

Nikkeiren (1995) *Shinjidai no Nihonteki Keiei* (Japanese management in a new era) (Tokyo: Nikkeiren).

Nonaka, I. and N. Takeuchi (1995) *The Knowledge-Creating Companies* (Oxford: Oxford University Press).

Shirai T. (1992) *Gendai Nihon no Romukanri* (HRM in contemporary Japan), 2nd edn (Tokyo: Toyo Keizai Shimposha).

4
Employment Adjustment since the Financial Crisis

Michio Nitta

Since the collapse of the bubble economy in Japan it has become common to hear talk of growing labour mobility, and it is even argued that Japanese employment practices have undergone a fundamental transformation. However it is more accurate to say that Japanese-style employment practices have continued to function as they have always done and labour market adjustments have only gradually been implemented (Nitta, 1998). Moreover the pace of employment adjustment has been significantly slower than it was during the recessions that followed the first oil crisis in the mid 1970s and the extreme appreciation of the yen after the Plaza Accords in the mid 1980s. This slower pace has probably been influenced by memories of the labour shortage during the bubble period and widespread expectation of economic recovery.

Nevertheless between 1997 and 1998, beginning with the failure of the Hashimoto government's policies, a financial crisis developed with eventual world-wide repercussions, and with the subsequent failure of major securities companies and banks both the pace and the nature of employment adjustment began to change markedly. While it would be premature to say that Japanese employment practices will be radically transformed or entirely replaced, unforeseen developments can be observed in a number of spheres. Moreover problems that have recently arisen will be extremely difficult to resolve solely by means of previous methods.

Employment adjustment in response to economic change

The percentage of establishments (manufacturing and wholesale/retail) that implemented employment adjustment measures in 1973–2002 is shown in Figure 4.1. In line with the economic cycle, the percentage

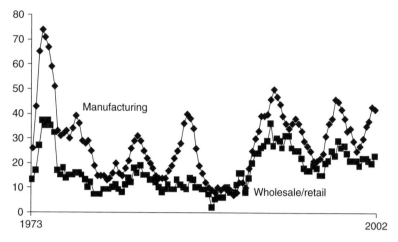

Source: Ministry of Health, Labour and Welfare (2003).

Figure 4.1 Percentage of establishments that took employment adjustment measures, 1973–2002

increased after 1997 and peaked in 1999, and thereafter decreased as the economy stabilized. Then in 2001 it increased in response to the economic stagnation caused by the recession in the information technology sector and the terrorist attack on the United States.

According to standard Japanese employment practice, whenever possible working hours, are adjusted first in order to avoid personnel reductions. The greater part of the statistics shown in Figure 4.1 consisted of overtime reductions. Few enterprises resorted to the more extreme measures of voluntary redundancy or retirement. Even in the fourth quarter of 1993, the lowest point of the post-bubble recession, only 2 per cent of manufacturing firms and 1 per cent of retail companies invited voluntary retirement or redundancy. Prior to 1997 the highest this ratio had reached was 5 per cent in the manufacturing industry during the second quarter of 1975, which coincided with the lowest point of the recession that followed the first oil crisis.

Of note, however, is the steep rise in 1998. During 1997 in the manufacturing industry the ratio remained at 1–2 per cent in all four quarters, but in the first quarter of 1998 it rose to 2 per cent, in the third it rose to 3 per cent and in the fourth it rose to 4 per cent, going on to reach a peak of 7 per cent in the first quarter of 1999. This not only matched but also exceeded that witnessed after the first oil crisis. With economic stabilization the figure settled down to 2 per cent, but in 2001 it increased again, rising from 3 per cent in the first quarter to 5 per cent in the third, 8 per cent in the fourth and 9 per cent in the first quarter of 2002. In other words, close to one tenth of Japan's major manufacturing companies made workforce adjustments during that period. In light of the data in Figure 4.1, it would seem that companies' ability to adjust working hours had reached its limit, thus necessitating personnel reduction. It is also possible to interpret this as illustrating how the pressure to make employment adjustments steadily increased – especially among the so-called 'companies on the losing side' (*make-gumi kigyo*) – to the point where they became inevitable.

Termination of employment for business reasons

As the proportion of enterprises carrying out personnel adjustments by such means as voluntary retirement and redundancy increased, so too did the scale of the adjustments within companies. Workforce adjustment not only took place in the manufacturing and construction industries but also spread to the financial and insurance sectors, which had previously managed to avoid the practice. As shown in Figure 4.2 the percentage of personal reductions for business reasons increased sharply after the financial crisis of 1997–98. In 1999 the ratio reached

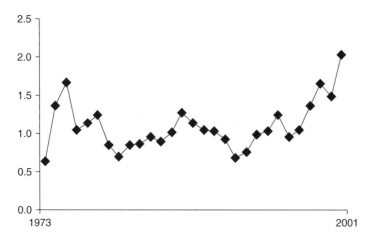

Source: Ministry of Health, Labour and Welfare (2002), *Labour Force Survey*.

Figure 4.2   Percentage of personnel reductions for business reasons, 1973–2001

1.65 per cent, on a par with the 1.66 per cent recorded in 1975 after the first oil shock, but by 2001 it had risen to a record high of 2.03 per cent.[1]

Unemployment

The consequence of these terminations was not only a rise in unemployment, but also prolonged spells of unemployment for those among the newly jobless who had been part of the labour force for sometime and for whom it was not easy to find alternative employment. As Figure 4.3 shows, the unemployment rate rose sharply from 3.4 per cent in 1997 to 4.1 per cent in 1998, 4.7 per cent in 1999 and 5 per cent in 2001. Of course these figures also include youths who were unemployed as a result of the structural adjustment of the labour market. Nevertheless the link between recession, workforce adjustment and high unemployment cannot be denied. As there appears to be little prospect of the situation improving in the near future, Japan's reputation as a nation of low unemployment would seem to be a thing of the past.

When the unemployment rate rises there is a concomitant increase in the number of persons receiving unemployment benefit. The number of persons who received the basic allowance jumped from 874,000 in 1997 to 1,021,000 in 1998, and the basic take-up rate (the ratio of persons

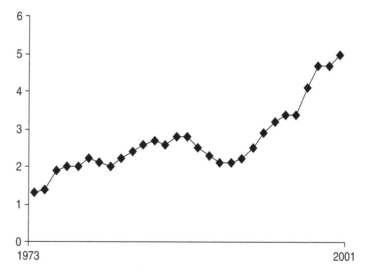

Source: Ministry of Public Management, Home Affairs, Posts and Telecommunications (2002a).

Figure 4.3   Unemployment rate, 1973–2001 (per cent)

receiving the basic allowance to the total number of insured persons) rose from 2.5 per cent to 3 per cent. As it is not inconceivable that the unemployment insurance funds might end up in deficit, steps must be taken to counter this trend.

The labour participation rate

From 1998 there was an upward trend in number of people leaving the labour market, having given up hope of finding work because of the deterioration of the economy. As was the case after the first oil crisis, when there had been a reduction in the number of female part-time workers, reductions in the labour participation rate concealed real rises in unemployment, thus enabling Japan to maintain its low official unemployment rate. Between the collapse of the bubble and 1995 there had been a slight decrease in the labour participation rate but it was not unusually large. However between 1997 and 2000 the rate fell from 63.7 per cent to 62.0 per cent (Figure 4.4). As the labour force numbered roughly 67 million in 2001, a 1.7 per cent reduction in the labour

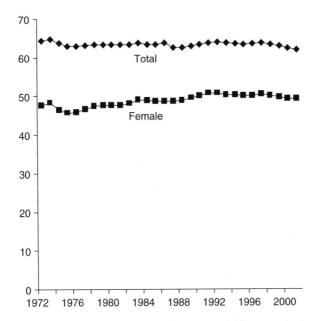

Source: Ministry of Public Management, Home Affairs, Posts and Telecommunications (2002a).

Figure 4.4 Labour participation rate, 1972–2000 (per cent)

participation rate amounted to a decrease of approximately 1,800,000 persons in the labour supply, constituting a considerable constriction of the workforce.

What distinguishes the falling labour rate since 1997 is the fact that, unlike after the first oil shock, it was not mainly female workers who were affected. While the female labour rate did drop by 0.6 per cent between 1997 and 2000, the male labour rate fell a full 2 per cent during the same period. Bearing in mind that the average male rates in 1997 and 2000 were 77.7 per cent and 75 per cent respectively, if we look at the trends among male workers according to age group, those that stand out are the 20–24 age bracket (with a fall from 75.0 per cent to 71.9 per cent), the 55–64 age group (85.1 per cent to 83.4 per cent) and those aged 65 and over (36.7 per cent to 32.9 per cent). The decline in the participation rate for the youngest age group may have been influenced by the growing number of young people going on to higher education. Nevertheless young and older males have been hit hardest by employment adjustment.

Working hours

While the financial crisis proved to be the catalyst for companies steadily reducing their workforce, whether it had a similar effect on working hours is another matter. Figure 4.5 shows that between 1997 and 1999 the average number of hours worked per employee per month decreased, as did again the number of regular working hours, which had remained constant in 1994–96. This may have reflected a re-emergence of the 'unintended work sharing' that had characterized the first half of the 1990s but close analysis of the monthly labour statistics published by the Ministry of Health, Labour and Welfare show clearly that the nature of the reduction in working hours in 1997–99 differed from that in the early 1990s, and that the difference lay in the growing use of part-time workers, as can be inferred from Figure 4.5.

Changes in the regular employment index (with 1995 as 100) show that while for full-time workers there was a 7.4 per cent increase between 1990 and 1995 (from 93.1 to 100), during the following five years there was a 3.7 per cent decrease (from 100.1 in 1996 to 96.4 in 2001). Conversely for part-time workers the index rose 22.0 per cent in 1990–95 (from 82.0 to 100) and a further rise from 104.6 to 126.1 in 1996–2001 (Ministry of Health, Labour and Welfare, 2002). These data may reflect the diversification of employment patterns, but they also show that the average working hours for full-time workers have

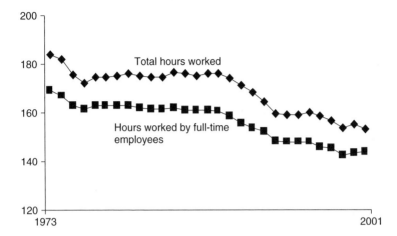

Source: Ministry of Health, Labour and Welfare (2002).
Figure 4.5 Average monthly working hours, 1973–2001

decreased due to the increasing proportion of part-time workers working shorter hours. It is likely that one outcome of this development was that the real pay per hour index, which had continued to rise until 1997, hit a ceiling and levelled off (Figure 4.6).

Conclusions

How should we interpret the employment adjustments made since the 1997–98 financial crisis? From the perspective of employment practices, are Japanese-style employment practices breaking down and being replaced by new ones?

This is not an easy question to answer. While the Japanese employment system was feted for the provision of lifetime employment, there was never actually a guarantee that employees would not be laid off. When the economic situation made employment adjustment inevitable, personnel cutbacks were initially avoided by adjusting working hours and then by reassigning or temporarily transferring personnel. However in the long term these measures reached their limit and voluntary redundancy and early retirement were introduced with a lump-sum redundancy payment being made to those who volunteered to leave the company. As the encouragement of voluntary retirement had been resorted to on previous occasions it is possible to view this simply as the

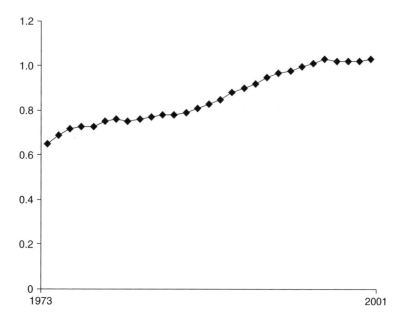

Source: Ministry of Health, Labour and Welfare (2002); Ministry of Public Management, Home Affairs, Posts and Telecommunications (2002b).

Figure 4.6   Index of real pay per hour, 1973–2001

efficient operation of Japanese employment practices in times of economic crisis. However compared with the situation in the early 1990s, this time the number of companies that engaged in personnel adjustment was larger and the speed at which employment adjustment progressed from working-hour adjustment to personnel adjustment was greater. This might suggest that employment practices are undergoing some kind of transformation. But even here, if the gentle pace of employment adjustment in the early 1990s is taken as abnormal in comparison with those in earlier recessions, it can be argued that the most recent adjustments simply represent the redressing of an outstanding imbalance.

The retirement benefit system provide a basic index by which Japanese employment adjustment practices can be systematically evaluated. If steps were taken to put an end to these schemes and the funds were absorbed into the monthly wage, it would be clear that a major systemic change had taken place. At present, however, few companies have taken this step, although far more are using their retirement benefit systems to implement workforce adjustments. In the event of an even worse economic crisis in the future it is uncertain whether companies would be able to continue to portray such measures as means to maintain lifetime employment for the remaining employees. Trust in the system would weaken and workers would no longer engage in the activities associated with lifetime employment (for example efforts to improve productivity and engagement in training aimed at increasing the company's human capital) and the practice would cease to have substantive meaning. In such a situation it is highly likely that managements would become more clinical about making workforce adjustments. This would pave the way for completely new employment practices. Of course things might never reach this stage and matters could be resolved by a partial revision of the system, such as increasing personal mobility by lowering the extent to which wages are determined by length of employment, or increasing flexibility by making more use of fixed-term employment contracts to create an employment system with a medium-term focus. After all the real world will remain in a state of flux.

Note

1. Included in these figures are temporary transfers and returns from transfer. In the long term the extent of transfers increased. However in the short term the percentage of transfers tended to decrease during the recession, showing that the sudden increase in the percentage of dismissals during this period was not the result of an increase in transfers.

References

Ministry of Health, Labour and Welfare (2002) *Monthly Labour Statistics* (Tokyo: Ministry of Health, Labour and Welfare).
Ministry of Health, Labour and Welfare (2003) *Survey of Labour Economic Trends* (Tokyo: Ministry of Health, Labour and Welfare).
Ministry of Public Management, Home Affairs, Posts and Telecommunications (2002a) *Labour Force Survey* (Tokyo: Ministry of Public Management, Home Affairs, Posts and Telecommunications).
Ministry of Public Management, Home Affairs, Posts and Telecommunications (2002b) *Consumer Price Index* (Tokyo: Ministry of Public Management, Home Affairs, Posts and Telecommunications).
Nitta, M. (1998) 'Employment Relations after the Collapse of the Bubble Economy', in J. Banno (ed.), *The Political Economy of Japanese Society, Volume 2: Internalization and Domestic Issues* (Oxford: Oxford University Press), pp. 267–84.

5
Convergence and Diversity: Emerging Patterns of Human Resource Management in Japan
John Benson

Introduction

That Japan was the economic success story of the second half of the twentieth century is undisputed. For most of this period Japan experienced substantial economic growth, driven primarily by the manufacturing sector. This growth is well illustrated by the success of the automotive industry. Between 1955 and 1982 the Japanese share of global motor vehicle production rose from just over 1 per cent to 30 per cent. Large Japanese automobile companies were not only significantly more productive than their American or European counterparts, but their products were also of a higher quality (Womack *et al.*, 1991). This trend was repeated in many other manufacturing sectors. By the mid 1980s Japanese companies had captured over 80 per cent of the world market for cameras, video recorders, and watches, over 70 per cent of the market for calculators and microwave ovens, and in excess of 50 per cent of the market for motorcycles and colour televisions (Oliver and Wilkinson, 1992).

This global success was supported by human resource management (HRM) based on internal labour markets and stable relationships between all stakeholders. Age-based wages and promotion, lifetime employment and strong worker commitment allowed companies to increase their market share while reducing unit costs and improving quality. However, the low rates of real economic growth during the 1990s, together with growing global competition, placed pressure on Japanese manufacturers to reconsider their HRM practices. Nikkeiren, the major employer body, proposed fundamental changes to the system of lifetime employment when it suggested that Japanese companies needed three types of employee to prosper: a core or 'elite' group of long-term employees; a 'contractor' group of specialists to deal with specific, usually short-term, problems; and a 'peripheral' group of employees to undertake simple, routine tasks on a non-permanent basis (Nikkeiren, 1995, 1999).

Yet reform of HRM practices is not a simple as Japanese HRM is embedded in the wider business system, institutions and social values (Whitley, 1992; Clegg and Kono, 2002). This contextual dependency means that change will generally be incremental and will initially involve experimentation rather than fundamental reforms to the system (Benson and Debroux, 1997; Benson, 1998). Even if there is a general move towards some idealized version of Western HRM, there may also emerge a diversity of practices amongst Japanese companies. Thus parallel trends of convergence and divergence may characterize the Japanese system during the period of experimentation and transition. On the other hand they may represent a temporary equilibrium position prior to an economic recovery that would prompt a return to the traditional HRM system.

It is clear from previous research that changes have occurred in Japanese HRM over the past decade. The first question addressed by this chapter is therefore not whether change has taken place but whether this change has extended to the basic HRM architecture. To make some assessment of the durability of the HRM reform the second question is what have been the key drivers of this change? The chapter begins with a brief outline of the postwar Japanese economy and a review of recent research. The limitations of this research are then discussed, including the failure to link the findings to the underlying economic factors. The subsequent section outlines the research propositions, details the methodology adopted and provides information on the market environment of the companies that took part in the research. The following two sections present the research results and explore the extent to which economic factors can explain the changes taking place in Japanese HRM. A short conclusion completes the chapter.

The economy, HRM and the Japanese company

The Japanese postwar economy

The postwar Japanese economy experienced substantial economic growth until the end of 1991. Economic growth of around 10 per cent ceased after 1970, although Japan's gross domestic product (GDP) grew by more than 5 per cent per annum over the next 20 years. This period was not one of constant growth, but of declining real GDP growth and a series of economic cycles. As the economy became larger, achieving high levels of growth became more difficult. Moreover much of the growth was achieved by expanding production and facilities. However, export limitations meant that sales could not grow in line with the increased production and so a lower growth rate was unavoidable (Nakamura, 1981). Unemployment during this period was low, fluctuating between 1 per cent and 2 per cent in the 1960s and 1970s and between 2 per cent and 3 per cent in the 1980s (Ito, 1993).

From the early 1990s the Japanese economy went into recession and for the remainder of the decade low rates of economic growth prevailed. Only in 1996 did real GDP growth reflect the conditions that had prevailed a decade earlier and much of this growth was due to substantial spending on government projects (*Nikkei Weekly*, 4 November 1996). Details are provided in Table 5.1. For an economy based on and accustomed, to high growth, this economic downturn had a serious effect on employment. In 1995 regular employment fell for the first time in 20 years and in manufacturing there was a fall of 1.9 per cent from the previous year (JIL, 1996). Unemployment, which had been 2.1 per cent in 1991, rose to 3.1 per cent by the end of 1995, and by December 2001 it had risen to 5.5 per cent (JIL, 2002).

Table 5.1 Japanese real GDP growth and unemployment, 1990–2002 (per cent)

	Real GDP growth	Unemployment
1990	4.8	2.1
1991	3.8	2.1
1992	1.0	2.2
1993	0.3	2.5
1994	0.6	2.9
1995	1.5	3.2
1996	5.1	3.4
1997	1.4	3.4
1998	−1.1	4.1
1999	0.1	4.7
2000	2.8	4.7
2001	0.4	5.0
2002	0.3	5.3

Sources: IMF (2002); Cabinet Office (2003).

HRM and the Japanese company

The sustained economic downturn over the past decade has led to a substantial decline in company performance. This, coupled with increased competition, has placed pressure on companies to restructure their HRM. Attempts are being made to link employee appraisal, remuneration and promotion more closely to company performance (Benson and Debroux, 1997; Wolfgang, 1997; Rebick, 2001; Dalton and Benson, 2002) and management's preferred employment strategies (Benson, 1998). A survey by Tokai Sogo Kenkyujo (2001) indicated some departure from promotion based on age and skill, although it did not appear to be based simply on job-related factors. Companies are increasingly linking pay increases to individual performance. There is some evidence that this individualization of remuneration has led to wider salary differentials for managers in larger companies (RIALS, 2000). Some companies have also introduced annualized remuneration schemes, but this practice tends to be restricted to managers (*Rosei Jiho*, 5 January 2002).

Modes of employment, as in Western economies, are also undergoing change. A study by the Japanese Ministry of Labour (1998) found a decrease in the number of regular, full-time employees and a corresponding increase in part-time and casual workers. The *Nikkei Weekly* (18 October 1998) reported a steady increase in the number of employees registered for temporary work. In addition there has been a decline in the commitment to lifetime employment (Lincoln and Nakata, 1997; Takahashi, 1997). Underpinning these changes have been demands by companies for more quantitative flexibility (Nikkeiren, 1999). Younger workers have contributed to these changes in that many wish to be promoted on skill and their pay to be merit based (Benson and Debroux, 1997). Moreover they are looking for improvements in the quality of life, more freedom to travel, and opportunities to undertake entrepreneurial activities and the chance to gain more international experience (*Nikkei Weekly*, 6 April 1998).

The greater market competition faced by Japanese companies has placed pressure on the traditional way of handling annual wage increases. Until 1998 *Shunto,* the national wage fixing process, was delivering real wage increases, although in declining amounts (JIL, 2000a). This paralleled the declining influence of unions (Tsuru, 1995) and unions' renewed emphasis on employment protection (Benson and Debroux, 2000; Kuwahara, 2000). The reduced union influence at the company level resulted in a decline in collective bargaining and companies expanded their joint consultative arrangements. By 1997, four out of five unionized companies had such mechanisms in place (JIL, 2000b). Now all issues but wages tend to be handled through joint consultation (Araki, 1996; JIL, 2000b; Koshiro, 2000).

The changes identified above have placed more emphasis on the performance of individual employees and their contribution to company performance. Will such changes lead, as suggested by Ornatowski (1998), to the end of the Japanese-style system of HRM? It is clear from the literature that most of the changes are at the experimental level and are restricted to managerial employees or certain groups of workers in large companies. It is also the case that change has been uneven, both within and between companies. This leads to the conclusion that some convergence towards the idealized version of HRM is taking place but that greater diversity in HR practices exists. There is little evidence that the changes constitute a strategic, integrated, policy-oriented approach to HRM or that they have been incorporated into the fundamental assumptions and principles underpinning the basic architecture of HRM.

A variety of factors have been identified as driving the changes, including the prolonged period of economic stagnation, a number of social factors (the ageing of the population, the declining birth rates, the short-term horizons of young people), the natural limits of the Japanese business system, globalization and the Asian financial crisis (Benson and Debroux, 2004). Yet little attempt has been made in the literature to understand what these factors mean for the stability of the HRM system and the sustainability of the changes. For example, there has been no consideration of whether the pressures will be short-lived and therefore will cease to be major drivers of change. This is clearly the case with the Asian financial crisis, which is no longer a major force for change.

The same could be said of the pressure for change generated by the poor state of the economy over the past decade or so. Would improved economic performance allow companies to revert to the well-tried and tested HRM model, or would social changes continue to exert sufficient pressure for a continuation or acceleration of the developments observed so far? The fact that the ultimate shape and direction of the changes are unclear has caused some commentators to suggest that the current Japanese model of HRM is both hybrid and contradictory (Benson and Debroux, 2003).

Research propositions, methodology and market environment

Research propositions

The focus of the remainder of this chapter is the degree and drivers of change in HRM. The research presented earlier in this paper suggested that while HRM change has taken place it has not extended into managerial labour strategy. In other words change is still at an experimental stage and has not penetrated HRM policy or its architecture. While the degree of change can be determined, the drivers of such change are more difficult to identify. Nevertheless one way of assessing the proposition is to test the hypothesis that the degree of enterprise change is greatest in periods of greatest economic difficulty. This implies that change should have been greatest in 1995, and to a lesser extent in 2001.

Methodology

The research was carried out between 1991 and 2001 in the Kansai region of Japan.[1] Although this region is not necessarily representative of Japan as a whole it is a traditional manufacturing centre and has a variety of industries and companies. The region has a population of over 21 million and at one time its gross domestic production accounted for nearly 3 per cent of world manufacturing production (OBA, 1991; OCCI, 1992; Osaka Business, 1996). The major employer group in the region is the Osaka Chamber of Commerce and Industry (OCCI). During the research period, the OCCI had about 39,000 members, of which just under 30 per cent were in the manufacturing sector. The research sample consisted of OCCI members engaged in manufacturing with a minimum of 100 employees. Restricting the sample to companies of this size meant that a range of companies, as measured by union presence and a variety of management practices, would be represented in the sample.

Questionnaire surveys were conducted in 1991, 1995 and 2001. The questionnaire covered a range of issues, including product markets, company performance, union activity, organizational change, payment systems and employee consultation. The questionnaire was developed in conjunction with a number of Japanese academics, the Japanese Confederation of Trade Unions, the OCCI and the Kansai Employers' Federation (KEF). The translation into Japanese was carried out by a commercial translating company and was checked by the OCCI, the KEF and two Japanese scholars. The questionnaire was mailed to the chief executives of the selected companies in October 1991, October 1995 and January 2001. Accompanying the questionnaires were a letter from the researcher detailing his background and the objectives of the study, and a letter from the managing directors of the OCCI and the KEF stating their support for the research and encouraging companies to participate. The response rates for the three surveys were 26.1 per cent, 16.0 per cent and 19.5 per cent respectively. There were 253 useable responses in 1991, 172 in 1995 and 184 in 2001.

The resulting data enables the degree of change to be measured, using 1991 as the reference point. As the economy was still strong at that time (see Table 5.1), comparisons with this date allow the impact of the recession on HRM to be assessed. The data will also enable an examination of whether HRM change was universal or was being undertaken by poor performing companies or by companies operating in more competitive markets. This may reveal some of the reasons for the change and the growing diversity of Japanese HRM practices. Finally, the data enables a more refined analysis that incorporates aspects of company and union strategy. However, the data have certain limitations that restrict the generalizeability of the findings. Apart from the limitations imposed by the location of the research and the size of respondent companies, the three samples may not be entirely comparable as a proportion of the 1991, 1995 and 2001 samples contained different companies. Nevertheless there were no major differences between the three samples in terms of company age, number of workplaces, workforce size, manufacturing sector and labour costs, so some confidence can be placed in the analysis. The details are presented in Table 5.2.

Market environment

As discussed earlier, in the 1990s there was a weakening of the Japanese economy, with low levels of economic growth and rising unemployment. What did these macroeconomic conditions mean for the manufacturing companies in this study? Table 5.3 presents details of a number of company-level economic indicators collected in the surveys. Product markets had become increasingly competitive with over half of the respondents claiming that competition in their principal product market was highly competitive. By 2001 price was rated more highly than quality as the most crucial factor in company success by nearly one in four companies or double the number in 1991. Meeting customers' demands was rated as the most important factor by just under half of the respondents, or much the same as in 1991. Product demand had

Table 5.2   Characteristics of the companies in the surveys

Characteristics	1991[1]	1995[2]	2001[3]
Average age of company (%)			
Less than 20 years	5.2	2.9	4.9
20–50 years	58.3	62.8	38.7
50 years or more	36.5	34.3	56.4
Average number of workplaces (%)			
Up to 5	49.2	52.0	45.8
6–10	26.6	25.7	25.4
More than 10	24.2	22.2	28.7
Average number of employees			
Full-time	531.1	491.2	524.6
Part-time	47.6	38.0	51.0
Manufacturing sector (%)			
Textiles, footwear and clothing	13.7	11.2	7.6
Chemicals/petroleum	18.2	14.7	12.0
Metal products	10.9	12.4	15.2
Machinery parts	9.7	11.2	8.7
Electrical goods	10.1	6.5	12.5
Other	35.4	44.0	44.0
Labour costs (% of total costs)			
Up to 20%	27.4	31.9	28.8
21–40%	41.3	41.2	37.7
More than 40%	31.3	26.9	33.6

Notes:
1. Number of responses ranged from 237 to 250.
2. Number of responses ranged from 159 to 170.
3. Number of responses ranged from 144 to 184.

contracted substantially for over a third of companies, a fourfold increase since 1991. More companies reported excess capacity in 2001 than in 1991. This had resulted in lower company profits. Management assessment of their companies' productivity *vis-á-vis* others in the industry remained fairly constant over the period.

There was a high degree of consistency between the market conditions (competition, demand) and company performance (profits, productivity) in the three years. When product market competition was high, this was associated with lower demand, lower profits and lower productivity. However, only in 1995 were these correlations statistically significant ($p < 0.05$), although in the latter case the relationship was also significant in 1991 ($p < 0.05$). Higher demand was associated with higher profits and higher productivity in all three years ($p < 0.01$). Finally,

Table 5.3   Product markets and company performance, 1991–2001 (percentage of companies)

Criteria	1991[1]	1995[2]	2001[3]
Product market			
Very competitive	41.9	47.7	56.0
Reasonably competitive	53.2	50.6	43.5
Not competitive	4.8	1.8	0.5
Crucial factor for success			
Price	10.7	18.2	22.4
Quality	24.6	20.6	13.7
Meeting customers' demands	42.6	34.7	44.8
Distinctive product	16.0	13.5	12.0
Product demand			
Expanding	30.0	18.2	15.9
Stable	61.1	50.0	47.5
Contracting	8.9	31.8	36.6
Operating at full capacity	78.8	63.2	67.1
Rate of return on capital (> 5%)	46.3	31.5	34.8
Productivity			
Much higher	4.0	6.0	7.1
A little higher	34.3	29.2	29.7
About the same	39.9	38.1	43.2
A little lower	20.2	25.0	17.4
A lot lower	1.6	1.8	3.0

Notes:
1. Number of responses ranged from 237 to 250.
2. Number of responses ranged from 159 to 170.
3. Number of responses ranged from 144 to 184.

higher productivity was associated with higher profits and this correlation was statistically significant in 1991 and 2001 ($p < 0.01$). Overall, for the companies in the study, product market conditions were significantly related to economic performance.

Reform of Japanese HRM

To test the first proposition, this section will explore the types of HRM practices that existed in the surveyed companies in the three years in question. The focus will be on a range of employment practices and enterprise-level collective bargaining. This will give some indication of the degree of change over time, although much of this change may have been the result of experimenting with new HRM approaches and therefore these practices may have been superficial and short-lived. To explore the depth of change the focus will then shift to managerial labour strategies. Changes in managerial strategies reflect a change of corporate ideology, and therefore reform of the basic HRM architecture.

HRM practices

HRM practices in place at the companies studied are presented in Table 5.4. Three employment practices declined over the years: quality circles, management-employee committees and management–union committees. Suggestion schemes and regular meetings with employees also underwent a substantial decline between 1991 and 1995, but slightly increased between 1995 and 2001. In contrast the use of just-in-time doubled between 1991 and 2001. Overall, with the exception of suggestion schemes, these HRM practices existed in less than half of the respondent companies by 2001.

Table 5.4   Employment practices, 1991–2001 (percentage of companies)

Practice	*1991*[1]	*1995*[2]	*2001*[3]
HRM practices			
Quality circles	65.5	58.8	49.4
Just-in-time	8.7	16.1	17.7
Suggestion schemes	80.4	73.1	75.0
Regular meetings with employees	60.8	48.7	49.1
Management–employee committee	52.7	46.6	42.9
Management–union committee	62.0	51.4	49.3
Internal labour market			
Lifetime employment[4]	65.9	56.8	56.4
Permanent employees[5]	88.5	88.0	85.7
Remuneration practices			
Bonuses[6]	5.1	4.6	4.1
Performance-related pay	50.6	41.0	46.0
Percentage of employees pay	12.5	12.4	17.6
Percentage of employees covered	44.1	43.4	46.1

Notes:
1. Number of responses ranged from 223 to 251.
2. Number of responses ranged from 148 to 169.
3. Number of responses ranged from 154 to 178.
4. Managers' assessment of the importance of lifetime employment to company performance (important or very important).
5. Percentage of total employment.
6. Equivalent months' pay.

Managers' assessment of the importance of lifetime employment to company performance also declined during the research period, with the vast majority of the decline occurring in the period 1991–95. However, this appeared to have had little effect on the number of permanent employees, as over 85 per cent of employees were classified as such. Bonuses fell notably over the period: from an average of 5.1 months' pay in 1991 to 4.1 months' pay in 2001. The use of payment schemes with some element of individual performance also declined in the first part of the decade, although it increased again between 1995 and 2001. More importantly, in the latter period both the amount of pay at risk and also the number of employees covered by such schemes increased.

While not all these changes were substantial, a clear trend is evident. Practices that involved high levels of participation declined, while more production-oriented practices such as just-in-time increased. Similarly, while companies' regard for the value of lifetime employment declined the actual percentage of permanent employees remained unaltered. Finally, attempts to link individual performance to pay declined a little while the percentage of an employee's pay at risk increased. The trend therefore appears to be towards the adoption of 'harder' HRM practices at the expense of 'softer' more employee-oriented ones.

Enterprise collective bargaining

The number of companies with a union presence declined during the period in question and especially in the first half of the 1990s. This paralleled the overall decline in unionism in Japan in 1990–2002, when union density fell from over 36 per cent to 20 per cent (JIL, 2003; Ministry of Health, Labour and Welfare, 2003). Those manufacturing companies where unions continued to exist the level of enterprise bargaining and the issues addressed in that bargaining did not change significantly over this period. The survey results are presented in Table 5.5.

The results reveal some interesting characteristics. First, traditional areas of union bargaining remained important, such as basic pay determination, bonuses, allowances and working conditions, including hours of work and overtime. In these areas there was little change between 1991 and 2001. Second, several areas of bargaining that posed a challenge to managerial prerogatives (new technology, staffing levels, management practices) declined in 1991–95 but picked up again in 1995–2001. This suggests that the initial shock of the recession led to a reduction of the issues that were covered in the bargaining process as

Table 5.5 Union coverage and bargaining, 1991–2001 (percentage of companies)

Issue	1991[1]	1995[2]	2001[3]
Enterprise unions	58.2	52.1	51.7
Bargaining issues			
Wage increases	99.3	97.7	96.8
Bonuses	99.3	97.7	97.9
Allowances	90.8	87.1	87.0
Working conditions	94.4	91.9	92.4
Hours of work	92.3	88.1	89.4
New technology	24.1	12.1	21.6
Health and safety	76.1	60.0	70.7
Staffing levels	17.4	11.9	18.0
Management practices	17.4	9.6	19.3
Work practices	73.3	65.4	67.4
Job assignments	17.8	13.3	10.1
Overtime	69.1	64.3	69.2
Employee grievances	73.0	67.9	71.4

Notes:
1. Number of responses ranged from 132 to 146.
2. Number of responses ranged from 81 to 87.
3. Number of responses ranged from 88 to 94.

unions were prepared to support management in coping with the recession, but this was not an open-ended commitment. The one exception to this was bargaining over job assignments, which declined consistently over the entire decade.

Managerial labour strategies

To what extent were these practice-level changes integrated into the long-tem HRM strategies of companies, or what is referred to as the HRM architecture? Companies were asked what actions would be included in their strategies if the demand for their major product changed. For companies facing a decline in demand two actions stood out. First, they were likely to reduce the number of regular employees, temporary employees and subcontractors (Table 5.6). Second, in 2001, nearly a quarter of the respondents stated that they were prepared to cut the wages of their remaining workers. This represented a sixfold increase in the number of companies that were willing to consider such an action over the period 1991–2001.

Table 5.6   Labour strategies in the event of falling demand for major product, 1991–2001 (percentage of companies)

Strategy–decrease	1991[1]	1995[2]	2001[3]
Regular employees	15.7	39.4	37.2
Temporary employees	66.3	80.1	83.0
Hours worked	67.6	58.0	70.9
Employees' wages	3.7	6.6	22.8
Productive capacity	62.3	54.0	56.4
Subcontractors	76.4	82.6	86.9

Notes:
1. Number of responses ranged from 188 to 207.
2. Number of responses ranged from 136 to 149.
3. Number of responses ranged from 149 to 165.

Table 5.7   Labour strategies in the event of growing demand for major product, 1991–2001 (percentage of companies)

Strategy–increase	1991[1]	1995[2]	2001[3]
Regular employees	54.6	36.9	24.4
Temporary employees	56.3	60.0	73.8
Hours worked (overtime)	52.5	56.5	63.8
Employees' wages	43.5	32.6	21.1
New technology	92.4	90.1	89.7
Subcontractors	76.3	67.8	77.0

Notes:
1. Number of responses ranged from 193 to 211.
2. Number of responses ranged from 135 to 146.
3. Number of responses ranged from 152 to 165.

A similar picture emerged in the case of what strategies would be adopted in the event of an increase in demand for their major product (Table 5.7). First, companies were not likely to consider increasing the number of regular employees to meet their staffing needs, but would instead increase the number of temporary employees. Second, the idea of increasing employees' wages declined from a high of 43.5 per cent in 1991 to 21.1 per cent in 2001. Taken together, these findings are consistent with a move towards a core-peripheral employment model (Atkinson, 1985, 1987; Benson, 1996). This suggests that Nikkeiren's 1995 reform agenda (Nikkeiren, 1995, 1999) for the adoption of a 'core', 'contractor' and 'peripheral' group of employees may, to some degree, be entering into companies' managerial labour strategies.

Economic factors and HRM change

The previous section showed that changes to HRM practices took place during the 1990s and that in general these were incorporated into managerial labour strategies. This suggests a deeper and potentially more permanent reform of HRM practices and a convergence towards a more Western form of HRM. Hence the first proposition, namely that HRM change has not extended into managerial labour strategy, must be rejected. In short, important changes have occurred in HRM policy and architecture. However, not all companies have reformed their HRM practices, so a greater diversity of HRM practices now exist in Japan.

According to the data gathered, the major period of change was 1991–95, when GDP growth averaged 0.85 per cent. This was in sharp contrast to the situation in 1986–91 when GDP grew at an average of 5.3 per cent per annum. In 1996–2001 HRM changes continued, although not to the same degree as in the earlier period, and in some cases there was a return to the situation at the start of the decade.

Part of the reason for the slowdown in change in the latter period was that GDP growth averaged 1.67 per cent. This represented a doubling of economic growth and meant that companies were now operating in a more positive economic environment. They had achieved slight improvements in productivity, orders and return on capital, although by that time markets had become more competitive, demand was falling and price was becoming increasingly important. As these latter factors were mostly external to the company they could not be addressed solely by the reform of HRM practices. Indeed for many manufacturers the answers lay in relocating part of their manufacturing operations overseas, particularly in countries where labour costs were low. Hence it appears that if the economic factors were the key drivers of this change then HRM changes would be more prevalent around 1995 than in 1991 and 2001.

One way to test this assertion is to examine the relationship between a range of company changes (new products, new technology, company structure, HRM practices and management) and economic and market factors. As can be seen in Table 5.8, the percentage of companies reporting recent changes increased in 1995, with the exception of new equipment. In this case the difficult economic times meant that fewer companies had the necessary capital to invest in new equipment so they

Table 5.8   Organizational changes, 1991–2001 (percentage of companies)

Type	1991[1]	1995[2]	2001[3]
New products	53.4	61.1	60.0
New equipment	78.8	66.7	63.2
Company restructuring	57.8	68.9	69.5
HRM practices	20.9	24.1	30.4
Senior management	51.1	57.2	56.9

Notes:
1. Number of responses ranged from 230 to 240.
2. Number of responses ranged from 158 to 165.
3. Number of responses ranged from 168 to 174.

responded by introducing new products and reforming their company structure, HRM practices and management. By 2001 this trend had ceased and it was only in the area of HRM practices that the percentage of companies undertaking reforms increased. This suggests that whilst economic factors may have initially driven the changes this was no longer the case with HRM.

In order to test the impact of economic factors on HRM further, chi-squared tests were conducted for changes in HRM practices and five economic factors: productivity, profits, capacity utilization, product competitiveness and demand for the company's major product. Productivity ($p < 0.05$), capacity utilization ($p < 0.01$) and product competition ($p < 0.05$) were significantly related to changes to HRM practices in 1991, but with the exception of product demand ($p < 0.10$) in 2001, these variables were not significantly related to changes in HRM for either 1995 or 2001. Thus while there is some support for the second proposition with regard to new products and equipment, this does not extend to HRM. In other words, factors such as social and demographic changes may be more important drivers of HRM change.

Conclusion

The 1990s were difficult years for manufacturing companies in the Kansai region of Japan. HRM reform was evident and to an extent the reforms were extended to HRM policy. While economic factors were important drivers of some organizational change, this did not appear to be the case with HRM, particularly after 1995. Hence it is unlikely that the changes to HRM will cease when the economy recovers. Further research is required to ascertain precisely what is driving HRM reform. Clearly, as mentioned in the last section, social and demographic factors are important, but they are unlikely to explain the full story.

The implications of the findings presented in this chapter are three-fold. First, workers and their unions can expect further HRM changes. While this will force unions to defend some of the benefits that accrued over the many years of economic growth, it will provide them with the opportunity to demonstrate the value of union membership. This is of crucial importance as at present many workers see little benefit in join-ing or remaining in unions. Second, management will find themselves in a dilemma; as the process of change continues there is a real risk of alienating workers and destroying the trust and commitment that has built up over the years. Until recently these factors were seen as giving Japanese companies their competitive edge. Continuing their reform agenda while keeping workers on side will be an important determinant of their future success. Finally, for the government the decline of the manufacturing sector and the consequent rise in unemployment will place it under growing pressure to provide a social safety net. Clearly industrial and social policy cannot continue to be ignored.

Note

1. I would like to thank the Japanese managers who gave freely of their time to participate in the surveys, and the Osaka Chamber of Commerce and Industry for its ongoing support throughout the project. I also acknowledge the sup-port of the Japan Foundation, the Australian Research Council, the University of Melbourne and Hiroshima City University, which funded the various stages of the research. I would also like to thank Ikuno Sako for her assistance with the 1995 and 2001 surveys.

References

Araki, T. (1996) 'Developing Employment Relations Law in Japan. Part 12: Collective Bargaining and Collective Agreements', *Labour Issues Quarterly*, 31, pp. 19–24.

Atkinson, J. (1985) *Flexibility, Uncertainty and Manpower Management*, IMS Report No. 89 (Brighton: Institute of Manpower Studies).

Atkinson, J. (1987) 'Flexibility of Fragmentation: The UK Labour Market in the 1980s', *Labour and Society*, 12 (1), pp. 87–105.

Benson, J. (1996) 'Management Strategy and Labour Flexibility in Japanese Manufacturing Enterprises', *Human Resource Management Journal*, 6 (2), pp. 44–57.

Benson, J. (1998) 'Labour Management during Recessions: Japanese Manufacturing Enterprises in the 1990s', *Industrial Relations Journal*, 29 (3), pp. 207–21.

Benson, J. and P. Debroux (1997) 'HRM in Japanese Enterprises: Trends and Challenges', *Asia Pacific Business Review*, 3 (4), pp. 62–81.

Benson, J. and P. Debroux (2000) 'Japanese Trade Unions at the Crossroads: Dilemmas and Opportunities Created by Globalization', in C. Rowley and J. Benson (eds), *Globalization and Labour in the Asia Pacific Region* (London: Frank Cass), pp. 114–32.

Benson, J. and P. Debroux (2003) 'Flexible Labour Markets and Individualised Employment: The Beginnings of a New Japanese HRM System', *Asia Pacific Business Review*, 9 (3), pp. 55–75.

Benson, J. and P. Debroux (2004) 'The Changing Nature of Japanese HRM: The Impact of the Recession and the Asian Financial Crisis', *International Studies of Management and Organizations*, 34 (1), pp. 32–51.

Cabinet Office (2003) *Economic and Fiscal Policy* (www.cao.go.jp).

Clegg, S. and T. Kono (2002) 'Trends in Japanese Management: An Overview of Embedded Continuities and Disembedded Discontinuities', *Asia Pacific Journal of Management*, 19, pp. 269–85.

Dalton, N. and J. Benson (2002) 'Innovation and Change in Japanese Human Resource Management', *Asia Pacific Journal of Human Resources*, 40 (3), pp. 345–62.

IMF (2002) *International Financial Statistics Yearbook* (Washington, DC: International Monetary Fund).

Ito, T. (1993) *The Japanese Economy* (Cambridge, Mass.: MIT Press).

Japan Institute of Labour (JIL) (1996) *Japan Labour Bulletin* (Tokyo: Japan Institute of Labour, April).

Japan Institute of Labour (JIL) (2000) *Japan Labour Bulletin* (Tokyo: Japan Institute of Labour, June).

Japan Institute of Labour (JIL) (2000a) *Japan Labour Bulletin* (Tokyo: Japan Institute of Labour, March).

Japan Institute of Labour (JIL) (2000b) *Japanese Working Life Profile 2000: Labour Statistics* (Tokyo: Japan Institute of Labour).

Japan Institute of Labour (JIL) (2003) *Japan Labour Bulletin* (Tokyo: Japan Institute of Labour, March).

Koshiro, K. (2000) *A Fifty Year History of Industry and Labor in Postwar Japan*, Japanese Economy and Labour Series No. 6 (Tokyo: Japan Institute of Labour).

Kuwahara, Y. (2000) 'The Future of the Labour Movement in Japan: Experiments and Possibilities', in *Proceedings of the 12th IRRA World Congress* vol. 3 (Tokyo: Japan Institute of Labour).

Lincoln, J. and Y. Nakata (1997) 'The Transformation of the Japanese Employment System: Nature, Depth, and Origins', *Work and Occupations*, 24 (1), pp. 33–55.

Ministry of Labour (1998) *White Papers on Labour 1998* (Tokyo: Ministry of Labour).

Ministry of Health, Labor and Welfare (2003) *Basic Survey of Trade Unions in 2002* (Tokyo: Japan Institute of Labour).

Nakamura, T. (1981) *The Postwar Japanese Economy* (Tokyo: University of Tokyo Press).

Nikkeiren (1995) *Nihonteki Keiei no Shin – jidai* (A New Era for Japanese – Style Management) (Tokyo: Nikkeiren Shuppanbu).

Nikkeiren (1999) *Keiei no Global ni Taiyo shita Nihongata* (The Japanese Style that Matched with the Globalization) (Tokyo: Nikkeiren Shuppanbu).

OBA (1991) *Osaka and Kansai: Financial and Economic Statistics* (Osaka: Osaka Bankers Association).

OCCI (1992) *An Economic Profile of Osaka* (Osaka: Osaka Chamber of Commerce and Industry).

Oliver, N. and B. Wilkinson (1992) *The Japanization of British Industry: New Developments in the 1990s* (Oxford: Blackwell).

Ornatowski, G. (1998) 'The End of Japanese-style Human Resource Management', *Sloan Management Review*, 39 (3), pp. 73–84.

Osaka Business Publisher's Council (ABPC) (1996) *Osaka: A New Gateway to Japan* (Osaka: Osaka Business Publisher's Council).

Rebick, M. (2001) 'Japanese Labor Markets: Can we Expect Significant Change?', in M. Blomstrom, B. Gangnes and S. LaCroix (eds), *Japan's New Economy: Continuity and Change in the 21st Century* (Oxford: Oxford University Press), pp. 120–41.

Research Institute for Advancement of Living Standards RIALS (2000) *Keieisha Enquete Chôsa no Gaiyô* (Summary of Survey on Corporate Governance), paper presented at the Twelfth IIRA World Congress, Tokyo, 1 June, pp. 20–8.

Takahashi, Y. (1997) 'The Labour Market and Lifetime Employment in Japan', *Economic and Industrial Democracy*, 18 (1), pp. 55–66.

Tokai Sogo Kenkyujo (Tokai Research Institute) (2001) *Jinji Seido no Genjo to Kongo no Kaizen no Hokosei* (Present Situation of the Human Resource Management System and the Directions of Change) (Tokyo: Tokai Sogo Kenkyujo).

Tsuru, T. (1995) 'Trade Unions in Contemporary Japan and Apathy of Union Members', in T. Inoki and Y. Higuchi (eds), *Employment and Labour Markets in Japan* (Tokyo: Nihon Keizai Shimbunsha), pp. 123–39.

Whitley, R. (1992) *Business Systems in East Asia: Firms, Markets and Societies* (London: Sage).

Wolfgang, L. (1997) 'Japanese Management Evolves Again', *Management Review*, 86 (6), pp. 36–9.

Womack, J., D. Jones and D. Roos (1991) *The Machine that Changed the World* (New York: Harper Perennial).

6
Decision-Making in Japanese Companies

Markus Pudelko

Introduction

Japanese management practices are currently undergoing major change in response to a significant loss of competitive edge. This chapter analyses the degree to which this also holds true for decision-making in Japanese companies. The analysis starts with an examination of what might be called the traditional practices in Japanese corporate decision-making; that is, those which were the norm during the heyday of the Japanese model from the 1980s until the early 1990s. The rationale for this approach is that any transformation can only be fully understood if first the object that actually is about to change is well known. Using a description of the traditional practices of Japanese corporate decision-making as a basis, their strengths and weaknesses will subsequently be analyzed. Strengths and weaknesses of these practices will be judged according to the following criteria: speed of decision-making and implementation, acceptance of and support for decisions taken, the ability to embrace new directions, transparency, accountability and motivational effects. Next, changes in the internal and external environment that are considered important factors in the transformation of Japanese corporate decision-making will be outlined. Finally the transformation process itself will be discussed and suggestions offered on how decision-making should change in order to lay the ground for the re-establishment of the competitiveness of Japanese companies.

The decision-making context

Four relatively closely related terms are often employed to describe the decision-making process in Japanese companies: 'collective', 'participative', 'consensus-oriented' and 'bottom-up'. According to Hofstede (2001), Japan scores low on individualism and correspondingly high on collectivism. This suggests also that decision-making in Japan is rather collectivist and conciliatory (Dore, 2000). Japan also scores very high on uncertainty avoidance, indicating that the Japanese are highly risk averse in their decision-making. This applies both to corporate strategies (Porter *et al.*, 2000) and to individuals' decision-making behaviour (Hofstede, 1983). Japanese employees rarely make bold proposals because they are reluctant to expose themselves to the possibility of criticism and loss of face. Consequently Hofstede's (2001) scores for individualism and uncertainty avoidance provide the cultural backdrop for the rather collective nature of decision-making in Japan.

Collective decision-making clearly has certain advantages, but only in particular circumstances. The context in which decisions are taken in Japanese companies therefore merits some consideration. It is argued here that collective, participative and consensus-oriented decision-making can only be understood against the background of lifetime employment, which has been typical in large Japanese companies. Even though lifetime employment is on the decline and more flexibility is being sought in respect of mid-career recruitment and the release of personnel, it still dominates corporate thinking at least as an ideal (Matanle, 2003) and it remains more prevalent than in the West (Pudelko, 2004a, 2005). The assumption that employees will spend their entire working life together with their colleagues reinforces their willingness to compromise and find a consensus. The desire for harmony, arguably one of the most prominent characteristics of Japanese culture and mentality, ensures that collective decision-making is not brought to deadlock by individuals trying to push through their own ideas (Ouchi, 1981). This is not to say that in Japanese society the pursuit of individual interests is unknown, just that it is dealt with differently. Individual interests are frequently achieved not by going against the group but through the group by promoting, at least on the surface, group objectives. Open conflict is usually suppressed. Vagueness in communication, negotiation and decision-making is important in this regard.

Along with lifetime employment, the seniority principle is an important contextual factor in Japanese decision-making and both are core elements of the traditional Japanese management model. Yet because of Japanese companies' efforts to adapt to the changing business environment the seniority principle is like lifelong employment, significantly in retreat. Western, and in particular American, management with its focus on performance serves as an important model in this respect (Pudelko, 2005).

Nonetheless when compared to Western organizations, seniority still remains significant in Japan. Due to the seniority principle senior employees do not feel that their career advancement is threatened by suggestions from younger colleagues. Moreover in order to be considered a good superior it is important to support subordinates' initiatives and include them in the decision-making process (Dore, 1973). Finally, lifetime employment and the seniority principle favour decisions with a long-term planning horizon for long-term growth rather than short-term profits, as both job security and promotion depend heavily on the growth of the company.

Job rotation – as a third typical Japanese human resource management instrument – aids understanding of the overall corporate philosophy and the specific objectives of the various departments. This in turn further facilitates collective, participative and consensus-oriented decision-making. Finally, the very thorough training provided to all members of the core workforce of large companies throughout their working life provides the necessary formal skills for participating in bottom-up decision-making (Tayeb, 1995).

Decision-making authority and accountability

The *de facto* delegation of decision-making authority can be viewed as typical for Japanese corporations. However as Arvey *et al.* (1991) argue, formal decision-making authority remains with the superiors. Lincoln (1989) points out the irony of the fact that Japanese managers tend formally to accept responsibility for wrong decisions that have in reality been taken by subordinates. This is the reverse of the situation in American companies, where subordinates are often blamed for wrong decisions taken at the top. Thus for Arvey *et al.* as well as Lincoln, formally centralized decision-making authority is linked to informally decentralized decision-making.

As promotion under the traditional seniority system depends less on performance than on length of employment, decision-making is often entrusted to young but able employees whose informal decision-making authority is not yet reflected in their official status. Hence decision-making authority is not necessarily congruent with hierarchical level. According to Aoki (1988) this decentralized decision-making structure, combined with a centralized organizational structure for incentive purposes, contrasts with Western management, which is characterized by centralized, hierarchy-determined decision-making and a decentralized, incentive system based on market forces (promotion and pay according to performance).

Rehfeld (1995) adds that in Japanese companies sanctions for wrong decisions usually start at the top and work their way down, not the other way round. In traditional Japanese companies, top managers have little more than representative functions as the real decision-making power lies collectively with middle managers. As will be shown, this situation is changing and top managers are becoming more proactive. Yet top managers still accept responsibility for decisions taken lower down and if necessary will resign. This provides middle managers with a substantial degree of security when taking decisions as they know they will not be held solely responsible for a wrong decision, and their superiors will shield them from criticism if possible. On the other hand it puts them under considerable pressure to show themselves worthy of their superiors' trust. If they make a wrong decision that gets their superiors into trouble the shame affects them as well.

When an individual makes a mistake the group will try to correct it, and even serious blunders are often met with lenience (Reinhold, 1992). Given the practice of job rotation it is probably inevitable that mistakes will occur, as employees continuously have to acquaint themselves with new positions. If a superior is assigned to a job with which he (core workers are invariably male) is unfamiliar, it is a matter of course for his subordinates to prevent him from making mistakes. In the light of this leniency towards mistakes, top managers often enjoy an almost unassailable position – as long as no public outcry occurs they can make one grave mistake after another without having to fear sanctions (Sullivan, 1992). The traditional focus on long-term growth and the comparative neglect of short-term profits has certainly contributed to top managers' lack of accountability for underperformance.

Due to the inclusion in the decision-making process of a multitude of employees from a variety of departments, it is hardly possible to attribute the success or failure of a decision to a specific individual or department. As employee assessments are traditionally more oriented towards decision-making behaviour and less towards concrete results the attribution of success is not of great importance. What matters is the success of the company, and this depends on the joint effort of all company members, not that of a specific department or individual. Consequently controllers, profit centres and internal transfer prices are often non-existent in Japanese companies.

The role of the superior

According to Ballon (1992) the most important quality in Japanese managers is the ability to interact with people, and the easiest way to access this is to observe how they influence decision-making. Encouraging active participation by all those involved in the decision-making process is considered by the Japanese to be extremely important. Superiors obtain detailed information through extensive discussions with those subordinates who have better knowledge of the issue in question. In turn, the subordinates take advantage of their superior's greater experience. Involvement in decision-making is also part of subordinates' training and development, which as noted above is considered to be very important in Japanese companies. Hence both the collective learning process and that of the individual are affected by the decision-making process. Kono and Clegg (2001) describe the Japanese company as a 'learning bureaucracy', a highly structured organization in which the virtues of learning, mutual information sharing and decision-making are deeply embedded.

Superiors often take what seems to Westerners to be a surprisingly passive role in group decision-making. They often remain silent and act more like mediators, rather than guiding the process and leading the discussions. Most of the talking is done by the superior's assistant, who is the second-ranking person. In the meantime the superior carefully observes the subordinate's decision-making behaviour. These observations form a central part of the employee's assessment therefore influence promotion decisions. This close control stands in contrast to the delegation of decision-making to autonomous working groups in European countries (Morishima, 1995).

The distribution of decision-making authority

An important characteristic of the traditional decision-making process in Japanese companies is that it starts at a comparatively low level of the company hierarchy and moves up the echelons. The idea underlying this bottom-up approach is that the initiative for a decision should come from the hierarchical level that is closest to the problem in question. Moreover the integration of lower-ranking managers into the decision-making process has a motivational effect. Hilb (1985) describes bottom-up decision-making as follows: lower-level managers serve the initiative and implementation function ('the problem identifiers'), middle-level managers structure and organize the initiative and later the implementation ('the moulders'), and higher managers provide support and encouragement ('the facilitators'). This is in stark contrast to the typical top-down decision-making in the West, where top managers plan and decide ('the planners'), middle managers control ('the controllers') and those on the lower hierarchical level implement ('the doers').

According to Ballon (1992) it is typical in Western companies to differentiate clearly between management (subdivided into lower, middle and top managers), which takes decisions, and the rank and file workers who implement them. In Japan, on the other hand, all employees from top managers down to shopfloor workers have their own decision-making competences. The decision-making authority of employees on the lower hierarchical levels (*ippan sha-in*) is mainly limited to operational issues, and particularly those concerning the production process. The precondition for this delegation of decision-making authority to the lower ranks is comprehensive training of all workers. Japanese companies typically invest substantially in the training of blue-collar workers so that they can solve problems autonomously as they occur. For example workers are authorized to stop the assembly line and bring the entire production flow to a halt in order to correct a fault immediately after it is discovered. By this means the number of specialized workers who are not directly involved in the production process, such as technicians, quality controllers and the repairers of products and production machinery, can be kept to the minimum.

Quality circles and suggestion systems for blue-collar workers, for which the Japanese management model is so famous, merit some attention in this context. Neither of the two should be regarded as instruments for reaching decisions autonomously as the suggestions and solutions put forward by these means have to be approved by engineers before implementation. However quality circles and suggestion systems are important means of stimulating ideas at low levels in the corporate hierarchy. Tapping workers' expertise while enhancing their motivation can be considered a genuine innovation of the Japanese management model.

Employees in the middle hierarchical levels (*kanri-sha*) coordinate the tasks of the *ippan sha-in* by cooperating closely with them. This cooperation is facilitated by the workplace layout. Superiors and subordinates share a large open office and on the production site production engineers have their desks directly next to the assembly line. The section chiefs (*kachos*) have a central role in decision-making processes as they are placed at the crucial intersection where all problems come together. Therefore they also have the heaviest workload. The delegation of decision-making authority from top management to the middle management level implies a more collective decision-making process as well. As there are many more *kachos* to whom decision-making authority is delegated than there are, say, board members who have delegated this authority, it is probably more accurate to speak of the distribution of decision-making authority than of the delegation of that authority.

Top managers (*keiei-sha*) are concerned with decisions of strategic relevance, but they often limit their involvement to setting out the general strategy and then leave it to middle managers to implement it in day-to-day business, intervening only in the event of severe problems.

Japanese executives might hold job titles that are comparable to those of their counterparts in the West, but their decision-making autonomy is much more limited. It is considered an important responsibility of top executives to respond actively to suggestions from below. This does not mean simply either accepting or rejecting suggestions, but asking further questions, stimulating additional suggestions and providing encouragement. Even CEOs will not make major decisions without extensively consulting their subordinates. In the rare cases where the CEO is the founder or owner of the corporation he may issue a 'proclamation of his own decision', but he would not fail to contact his subordinates afterwards to authorize that decision (Nishiyama, 2000).

Decision-making in Japanese companies is paralleled in the public sector. Here too real decision-making power often lies not at the very top – the prime minister or the cabinet – but in the hands of elite bureaucrats at the government ministries and agencies. It has been said that other countries possess a bureaucracy but the Japanese bureaucracy possesses a country. Inoguchi deprecatingly calls this type of government system 'karaoke democracy': 'One singer [or minister] comes on stage after the other, the melodies are always the same and they read the texts, written by others, from the teleprompter' (quoted in Sommer, 1998, p. 1).

Nemawashi and *ringi*

In Japanese companies bottom-up decision-making often follows a strictly formalized, if not ritualized, procedure called *ringi*, which can be translated as 'circulate a proposal, discuss and decide'. It is preceded by a long and informal discussion and consultation process called *nemawashi*, or 'twisting the tree roots around' in order to cut off disturbing roots (or objections) so that it can be easily uprooted. Decision-making is therefore based on a combination of informal and formal procedures. The sequence of *nemawashi* and *ringi* is as follows. When an important decision has to be taken, every manager who will be affected by the decision is involved in reaching it. This might result in the participation of up to 80 people. A team of about three younger employees from a lower managerial level (the *kiansha* or plan initiators) is assigned to collect the opinions of all 80 employees. Ideas and concerns can be voiced relatively freely at this stage, with no fear of committing oneself. The *kiansha* draft a proposal based on the results of this informal probing and submit it to each person involved. If the proposal is rejected it has to be replaced by another and the entire process starts again. This continues until a consensus is reached, thus concluding the *nemawashi* phase. A formal proposal is then drafted (the *ringisho*) and passed on, going from employees at the lowest up to the highest hierarchical level. Each time the managers put their official seal on the cover sheet of the document as a sign of their approval (signatures are not common in Japan). Once all 80 persons have formally approved the *ringisho* is passed on to the company's president. The decision is considered to have been reached when the latter has put his seal on it.

Middle managers have a key part in this process in that they help their younger colleagues to draft their proposals in such a way that they will meet the overall objectives and expectations of the top managers. The *kiansha* always have access to more experienced colleagues during this process and can move outside the official channels. Obtaining agreement involves a substantial amount of lobbying and persuasion. If resistance is met, third persons are enlisted to act as mediators, such as friends, golfing partners or graduates from the same university. Much of this lobbying is done over drinks, dinner or games of golf, rather than in formal meetings. Personal give-and-take-relationships can be of greater importance in this process than factual arguments about the decision itself (Nishiyama, 2000).

It should be added that collective decisions such as a *ringi* are virtually always unanimous. No votes are taken since that would divide the participants into the winning majority and the losing minority, which would harm the solidarity of the group. As Nishiyama (ibid., p. 121) puts it, 'Obtaining agreement from everyone is still the most widespread form of traditional decision making in Japan under almost all circumstances.' Hence decisions cannot be taken hastily to save time or meet deadlines. This does not mean, however, that all those participating in the process are in complete agreement with the final decision. Sealing the *ringisho* is more a declaration that individuals acknowledge that their opinion has been sufficiently considered in the decision-making process, and even though they might not fully agree with the decision they will ultimately give it their full support. In this way the almost impossible task of coming to complete agreement is avoided (Ouchi, 1981; Reinhold, 1992; Fürstenberg, 1993; Rehfeld, 1995). As everyone affected by a decision has been part of the decision-making process, their identification with it is enhanced and this is very important to the effective implementation of the decision.

The informal *nemawashi* process is of much greater importance in decision-making than the formal *ringi* since it is during *nemawashi* that the consent of all participants is mustered. Park (1995) therefore concludes that consultative management in Japan is largely founded on the principle of informalism. One might say that the *ringi* is less about finding a solution than confirming it.

Other characteristics of Japanese decision-making

Consensus decision-making obviously takes a significant amount of time. According to Rehfeld (1995), Japanese managers do not shoot from the hip, not even when the situation demands a quick shot. The many meetings that are needed to reach an agreement account for a substantial part of a manager's working day: the Japan Management Association puts the figure at about 40 per cent (Woronoff, 1992). Moreover these meetings usually only confirm what has already been decided informally through face-to-face consultation (Nishiyama, 2000). There will be little or no open discussion, expression of different opinions or raising of alternatives. Even constructive criticism would be considered a personal attack or an insult. While it is perfectly legitimate for Western managers to change their position during a meeting when confronted with new facts or arguments, in Japan this would be viewed as a serious social infraction and a betrayal of personal trust. Any agreement reached during an informal consultation is considered a firm commitment.

Drucker (1973) highlights another basic difference between Western and Japanese decision-making. Whereas in the West the focus is on the answer to a question (or its solution), for the Japanese the formulation of the question (or defining the problem) is more important. Therefore they first seek agreement on the right formulation of the question, as the right answer (or according to the Western conception, the actual decision) often follows automatically from this. By delaying the focused search for the solution to a problem, those participating in decision-making avoid committing themselves to a specific solution at an early stage as such a commitment would ensure that the final decision would be a victory for some and a defeat for others. The importance in Japanese culture of avoiding loss of face is particularly relevant here.

Furthermore as Rehfeld (1995) observes, Japanese decision-makers tend to look at any solution from different angles in order to identify possible long-term consequences. The same questions are asked again and again in this process, and through repeated examination of the questions the eventual decision gradually takes shape. This process continues until a general consensus is reached. More weight is given to qualitative or soft arguments and implicit information than to hard facts and explicit data. Expert systems and other IT-based planning and decision-making support systems are avoided as they are not considered able to handle the complexity of a decision problem.

Even during the decision-making phase attention is paid to its subsequent implementation. Japanese managers are mainly interested in the concrete execution of a decision and less concerned about its general rationality. Consequently the distinction between those who take decisions (the 'thinkers') and those who implement them (the 'doers') is not stressed. According to Ballon (2002) the conviction in Japanese companies is that it is not decisions that change reality, but their implementation. Furthermore in Japan it is less about reaching a decision (acting on reality) than about responding to imperatives (reacting to reality) (Ballon, 2005). In other words managers are less concerned about transforming reality through a conscious decision or creating a new reality than about adapting the company continuously to a changing reality. The execution of decisions and all those involved in this are therefore viewed as the basis for success, not excellent decisions or outstanding decision-makers. It follows from this that the flow of authority matters less than the flow of tasks and problems to be addressed. The distribution of information is also determined less by hierarchy than by intensive collaboration, developed over many years, among all those who are affected by the problem in question, irrespective of their hierarchical level. It is not explicitly formulated strategies that determine and regulate the decision-making process, but rather a network of information to which every company member contributes.

To sum up, whereas decision-making in the West can be described as individualistic, hierarchical, majority-oriented, top-down, linear, analytical, rational (systematic), abstract and focused, Japanese decision-making tends to be collective, participative, consensus-oriented, bottom-up, circular, systemic, intuitive (analogizing), concrete and holistic.

Evaluation

The complexity of the decision-making process and the effort involved in keeping a multitude of people on course mean that Japanese companies are very reluctant to make radical changes in direction. They tend to work intensively on the further development and refinement of a decision once it is reached, rather than dropping it and replacing it with a new one. A Japanese company can therefore be compared to a huge ocean liner that takes a long time to turn around, whereas American companies, with their much more centralized decision-making and more frequent changes of personnel, are more akin to speedboats. Rehfeld (1995) offers another image: Japanese managers are like dominoes – when they fall they all fall in the same direction.

It is not easy to reach a conclusive judgement of the Japanese decision-making process. While the relatively inflexible promotion system, based on the seniority principle, does not always result in the most competent employees occupying the higher managerial positions, the *ringi* system and other forms of participative decision-making permit talented employees with no formal decision-making authority to exert considerable influence on the decision-making process. Moreover, the initiative for a decision usually starts at the level closest to the problem, which appears to be an efficient way of improving specific processes incrementally. On the other hand employees on the lower hierarchical levels are often not sufficiently able to evaluate the consequences a decision will have for the company as a whole (Flynn, 1982). Participative decision-making may enhance the motivation of the workforce, but the effort of keeping the process harmonious carries the danger of not sufficiently valuing minority voices. Employees who hold a minority opinion thus tend to remain silent in order not to disturb the harmony. In the West self-expression and competitive behaviour are necessary if employees are to be noticed and valued, but the Japanese do not appreciate such behaviour. One might say that the Japanese do not hold outstanding persons in esteem as by definition they stand outside the group. The decision-making process therefore promotes passivity and obstructs creativity, radical innovation and new approaches. The ultimate decision is often hinted at from the start by higher managers. Hence the elaborate group decision-making process frequently only serves to confirm what has been decided well beforehand. Finally, group decision-making is characterized by ambiguity about responsibility, with everyone believing that someone else has the final responsibility and therefore no one actually takes that responsibility.

With regard to the acceptance of decisions, however, the Japanese system of decision-making certainly has advantages. Once a decision has been reached via the *ringi* procedure or another form of participative decision-making it is likely to be supported by all those involved. This is too important a point to be neglected as there are indications that support for a decision can be a more decisive factor in the success than the actual quality of the decision (Ouchi and Johnson, 1978). The ritual of the *ringi* also embodies the Japanese philosophy of cooperation in a much more direct way than the announcement of abstract, but possibly little respected, principles of employee participation.

The time it takes to reach a decision is closely connected with the time needed to implement it. As has been discussed, the decision-making process is both time-consuming and tiresome. The execution of the decision, in contrast, may take very little time as all the relevant information has been widely disseminated and the final decision does not have to be sold to those who carry it out as they have been involved in reaching it. There are frequent reports of Western managers complaining about the seemingly endless negotiations with their Japanese counterparts; and equally of Japanese businessmen criticizing the time it takes in Western companies to implement an agreed decision. Which of the two time criteria, that of decision taking or of decision implementation, ultimately prevails cannot be determined in general, but only for each single case.

One of the reasons why decision-makers in Japanese companies are able to cooperate harmoniously and reach consensus smoothly is their high degree of homogeneity. They all tend to be of Japanese nationality, male, have attended the same selection of top universities and have socialized over many years in the same company. While this homogeneity fosters harmonious decision-making which is very effective in incrementally improving standardized operations it renders any 'outside the box' thinking and more substantial changes of direction much more difficult. As Teramoto and Benton (2005) note, having a permanent group of decision-makers leads to information and knowledge stagnation and limits diversity. A dynamically changing environment, however, necessitates a steady influx of new agents with new ideas, viewpoints and expertise, not only for the innovation of products but also for the development of organizational processes, structures and strategies. For the sake of conflict suppression, radical or potentially controversial decisions are likely to be avoided. However in situations where paradigm shifts are called for, radical decisions are essential.

The unwillingness to deviate from established paths and venture along new ones is not restricted to companies but permeates the entire Japanese economy. According to Porter *et al.* (2000), Japanese companies' 'me-too' behaviour and unwillingness to differentiate their competitive strategies is a key weakness. They write:

> Although operational effectiveness can continue to be a source of competitive strength, it will not achieve superior performance on its own. Perhaps the most fundamental challenge facing Japanese companies is to embrace strategy, and begin the process of distinguishing themselves from rivals. Strategy requires hard choices about what *not* to do. In a nation where imitation has been the rule, companies need to either choose a set of activities that are *different* from competitors or perform activities *differently* than rivals do ... Being different is not a virtue in Japanese society ... The need to obtain so many approvals almost guarantees that bold or distinctive strategies will not be pursued ... But now Japanese companies must search for distinctive ways of competing, which requires a more creative, individualized process. (Ibid., pp. 162–3, 165)

Changes in the decision-making environment

It can be argued that during the boom years the Japanese decision-making process was on the whole perfectly adapted (internally) to the overall Japanese management model and (externally) to Japan's social and economic environment.

The internal contextual factors, to which the decision making was so well adapted, have already been discussed: lifetime employment, the seniority principle, job rotation, generalist career paths, intensive training, particularly for blue-collar workers and motivation through participation. As has been outlined, these cornerstones of the Japanese management model called for collective, participative, consensus-oriented and bottom-up decision-making. The latter reflected essential characteristics of Japanese society at large: collectivism, loyalty towards and identification with employers and colleagues, risk avoidance, a reluctance to take on individual responsibility, a circular and iterative approach to addressing problems, a preference for incremental steps rather than big leaps, and a strong desire to improve and perfect.

Corporate decision-making was not only very well adapted to the social environment but also to the economic context of the time when Japan attained its full economic power. This can be illustrated by the automotive industry, which probably symbolizes more than any other sector the rise of the Japanese economy and the effectiveness of the

Japanese management model in the 1980s. Japanese car manufacturers achieved something that their Western competitors considered impossible: improving product quality while at the same time reducing production costs, thus allowing a reduction in price. They achieved this not by breakthrough inventions or quantum-step management decisions, but by a myriad of incremental improvements in the quality of both the product and the production process. The focus on detail, quality circles, suggestion systems, the participation of the various departments and even of key suppliers in the decision-making process, and bottom-up decision making all helped to improve quality, cut costs and shorten the product cycle. In this mature and stable industry there was, until the 1990s, little need for radical changes. Hence the already established weaknesses of the Japanese decision-making process mattered relatively little.

By the mid 1990s, however, the economic environment had changed and Japan's high-growth economy had turned into one of virtually no growth. Because of the crisis in the financial sector, banks were unable to continue to finance long-term growth strategies with almost no concern for their profitability. While adopting 'me-too' strategies had been sufficient in the period of high growth, this could not guarantee survival in a stagnant economy. Globalization had taken away much of the stability that had shielded the Japanese economy and allowed for an insular and ethnocentric management approach. Competition had become more intense, the space of innovation and change had increased, and the demands in global markets had become more sophisticated due to the greater supply of information available to consumers and business customers. As a result of the collapse of the bank lending system, foreign investors substantially increased their shareholding in Japanese companies and demanded the implementation of global business standards.

Concentrating on pooling domestic strengths in order to build up competitive industries was no longer sufficient and competitors sought to combine their strength on a global scale via transnational value chains, strategic alliances, mergers, acquisitions and global financing. Even the automotive sector underwent significant change through cross-border mergers and acquisitions. Relatively new industries such as software and telecommunications became more important in national competitiveness, and the use of their products allowed dramatic increases in productivity across all business sectors. The development of new industries and the application of their products, however, necessitates creativity, originality, unconventional solutions, breakthrough innovations, risk taking and radical change.

With this substantial transformation of the economic environment the principal weakness of the Japanese management model in general, and the Japanese decision-making model in particular – the inability to respond rapidly and radically to change – became much more significant. Meanwhile the willingness of American companies to restructure their organizations and activities quickly and extensively was an important reason for the surge in their competitiveness in the 1990s.

Japanese decision-making has had to adapt to these new circumstances. Radical actions such as abandoning strategies, ceasing unprofitable activities, closing down departments and laying off personnel cannot be undertaken on the basis of collective, participative, consensus-oriented, bottom-up decision-making. Instead top managers have to adopt a much more prominent leadership role and find the courage to take decisions that may be unpopular with many employees.

According to Kono and Clegg (2001), top managers now play a much larger part in strategy formulation. However this should not be seen as a reversal of decision-making from bottom-up to top-down. As Kono and Clegg explain, strategies are increasingly being designed by top managers, but the details are then handed down to the individual departments for consideration of how the strategy might be implemented. Their proposals are ultimately returned to the top managers for discussion and approval. Thus the decision-making process is now U-shaped – descending from the top down through the ranks and then back to the top again. So instead of replacing the traditional Japanese decision-making process with the Western one, a synthesis of the two approaches has been adopted.

As discussed earlier, traditional Japanese decision-making is heavily interwoven with other aspects of management. It should therefore come as no surprise that any transformation of decision-making has entailed changes to other aspects of the management model. One such change is that increasing numbers of mid-career workers with special knowledge and expertise are being hired. In order to bring these high performers into decision-making positions, specialist career paths and performance-related promotion and pay are being introduced. In this regard accountability for decisions has to be increased so that employees can be better assessed for promotion or pay increases.

Globalization implies that decision-making in multinational companies should involve nationals from outside the company's country of origin, at least at the subsidiary level. However there is considerable empirical evidence that this is much less the case for Japanese companies than for companies from other countries. There are hardly any foreigners on the boards of Japanese companies, and even in foreign subsidiaries it is usually Japanese who make the key decisions (Kopp, 1999; Pucik, 1999; Beechler, 2005). Westney (1999) concludes that participation in decision-making must be extended to foreign nationals who are familiar with the Japanese way of doing things.

Empirical analysis

In order to investigate the still remaining differences between the Japanese and Western approaches decision-making, this section draws on a study by Pudelko (2000). As part of this study the heads of the human resource departments of the top 500 companies in Japan, the United States and Germany were asked to evaluate decision-making in companies in their own country. When asked whether their decision-making was mainly 'top-down' or 'bottom-up', the Japanese respondents replied that the emphasis was now slightly more on top-down than on bottom-up. This suggests that Japanese companies are indeed following a mixed strategy, as suggested above. Given the fact that bottom-up decision-making has been regarded as one of the key characteristics of Japanese corporate decision-making, this is a rather significant development. According to the survey results Japanese decision-making, however, is still far less top-down than it is in the United States and Germany.

When asked to rate their corporate decision-making behaviour between the poles of 'authoritative, individual decision-making behaviour where conflict is accepted' and 'participative, collective and consensus-oriented decision-making behaviour', the Japanese respondents were significantly more inclined towards the latter, in particular in comparison with the American and German respondents. Consequently it seems that little change has taken place in this regard.

Finally, the HR managers were asked to rank their decision-making practices between the following poles: 'tendency to base decisions on quantitative variables (hard facts)' and 'tendency to base decisions on qualitative variables (soft facts)'. There too, the Japanese respondents leant more towards the second response, although not strongly, while the US and Germany respondents stated that their companies focused more on quantitative variables. There seems to have been no significant change for these criterion either.

Overall the empirical analysis suggests there has been some change in Japanese decision-making practices, particularly in respect of the adoption of a more top-down approach, but other practices continue to lean more towards the traditional Japanese methods of decision-making.

Conclusion

At the beginning of this chapter, traditional decision-making in Japanese companies was characterized as collective, participative, consensus-oriented and bottom-up. Having analyzed actual practices in more depth, investigating in particular directions of possible change and referring to empirical survey data, the following conclusions can be drawn. Corporate decision-making in Japan now appears to involve far more guidance by top managers. As pointed out previously, this does not necessarily imply a complete reversal from bottom-up to top-down decision-making, rather that a synthesis of both approaches has evolved as bottom-up decision-making continues to be more represented in Japanese than in Western companies. There are also indications of a somewhat lesser degree of collective, participative and consensus-oriented decision-making than in the past. However, the differences from the more individual Western decision-making model remain significant. Participation, collectivism and consensus appear to be strongly embedded in Japanese culture and are therefore unlikely to be abandoned in the corporate world.

It has been suggested here that the objective of the transformation of the corporate decision-making process in Japan is to enable faster reaction to changes in the economic environment. This means that it is no longer possible to try to please everyone who will be affected by a decision (employees, customers, suppliers and retailers). Although companies have to respond to requests in order to generate profits, not all requests from all stakeholders can be treated equally. Instead choices and trade-offs have to be made about whose demands should be prioritized, which of their demands should be met and how this should be done. The challenge for Japanese companies appears to lie not so much in deciding what to do as in determining what *not* to do. Only by addressing this issue will Japanese companies be able to differentiate their strategies and shed their fixation with operational effectiveness. For this, corporate decision-making has to involve more creativity, originality and risk-taking. Decision-making autonomy, accountability and speed should be enhanced, and conformity and emphasis on the *status quo* should be replaced by more innovative and individualized decisions that might rock the boat and not meet everyone's approval. The focus should no longer be on improving a decision once it has been taken and continuing down the same path. Instead companies should monitor whether a decision is having the desired effect, and if it is not it should be abandoned and replaced by another. Incentives must therefore be geared more to rewarding initiative taking and less to the ability to follow others (including competitors). Decision-making should also involve the use of hard quantitative facts and IT resources in order to cope with the increasingly complex business environment and profit orientation.

While all these suggested changes imply the adoption of more Western-style corporate decision-making techniques, care must be taken to adapt them to the company's cultural, social and corporate context in order to avoid friction and frustration. Finding the right equilibrium between traditional practices and aspects of other management models is the key challenge faced by Japanese companies that wish to adapt to the changing competitive environment.

References

Aoki, M. (1988) *Information, Incentives, and Bargaining in the Japanese Economy* (Cambridge: Cambridge University Press).

Arvey, R. D., R. S. Bhagat and E. Salas (1991) 'Cross-Cultural and Cross-National Issues in Personnel and Human Resource Management: Where do we go from here?', in G. R. Ferris and K. M. Rowland (eds), *Research in Personnel and Human Resource Management. A Research Annual*, vol. 9 (Greenwich, CT, and London: JAI Press), pp. 367–407.

Ballon, R. J. (1992) *Foreign Competition in Japan. Human Resource Strategies* (London and New York: Routledge).

Ballon, R. J. (2002) 'Human Resource Management and Japan', *Euro Asia Journal of Management*, 12, pp. 5–20.

Ballon, R. J. (2005) 'Organizational Survival', in R. Haak and M. Pudelko (eds), *Japanese Management: The Search for a New Balance between Continuity and Change* (Basingstoke and New York: Palgrave).

Beechler, S. (2005) 'The Long Road to Globalization: In Search of a New Balance between Continuity and Change in Japanese MNCs', in R. Haak and M. Pudelko (eds), *Japanese Management: The Search for a New Balance between Continuity and Change* (Basingstoke and New York: Palgrave).

Dore, R. (1973) *British Factory–Japanese Factory* (Berkeley, CA: University of California Press).

Dore, R. (2000) *Stock Market Capitalism: Welfare Capitalism. Japan and Germany versus the Anglo-Saxons* (Oxford: Oxford University Press).

Drucker, P. F. (1973) *Management: Tasks, Responsibilities, Practices* (New York: Harper & Row).

Flynn, D. M. (1982) 'Japanese Values and Management Process', in S. M. Lee and G. Schwendiman (eds), *Japanese Management. Cultural and Environmental Considerations* (New York: Praeger), pp. 72–81.

Fürstenberg, F. (1993) 'Industrial Relations in Germany', in G. Bamber and R. D. Lansbury (eds), *International and Comparative Industrial Relations. A study of Industrialised Market Economies*, 2nd edn (London: Allen & Unwin), pp. 175–96.

Hilb, M. (1985) *Personalpolitik für Multinationale Unternehmen. Empfehlungen aufgrund einer Vergleichsstudie japanischer, schweizerischer und amerikanischer Firmengruppen* (Zurich: Verlag Industrielle Organisation Zürich).

Hofstede, G. (1983) 'The Cultural Relativity of Organizational Practices and Theories', *Journal of International Business Studies*, 14 (2), pp. 75–89.

Hofstede, G. (2001) *Culture's Consequences. Comparing Values, Behaviors, Institutions and Organizations across Nations*, 2nd edn (London and Thousand Oaks, CA: Sage).

Kono, T. and S. Clegg (2001) *Trends in Japanese Management. Continuing Strengths, Current Problems and Changing Priorities* (Basingstoke and New York: Palgrave).

Kopp, R. (1999) 'The Rice-Paper Ceiling in Japanese Companies: Why it Exists and Persists', in S. Beechler and A. Bird (eds), *Japanese Multinationals Abroad: Individual and Organizational Learning* (Oxford: Oxford University Press), pp. 107–28.

Lincoln, J. R. (1989) 'Employee Work Attitudes and Management Practice in the U.S. and Japan: Evidence from a Large Comparative Survey', *California Management Review*, 32 (1), pp. 89–106.

Matanle, P. (2003) *Japanese Capitalism and Modernity in a Global Era. Re-fabricating Lifetime Employment Relations* (London and New York: RoutledgeCurzon).

Morishima, M. (1995) 'The Japanese Human Resource Management System: A Learning Bureaucracy', in L. Moore and P. Jennings (eds), *Human Resource Management on the Pacific Rim. Institutions, Practices, and Attitudes* (Berlin and New York: Walter de Gruyter), pp. 119–50.

Nishiyama, K. (2000) *Doing Business with Japan. Successful Strategies for Intercultural Communication* (Honolulu: Hawaii University Press).

Ouchi, W. G. (1981) *Theory Z. How American Business Can Meet the Japanese Challenge* (New York: Avon).

Ouchi, W. G. and J. B. Johnson (1978) 'Types of Organizational Control and Their Relationship to Emotional Well Being', *Administrative Science Quarterly*, 23 (2), pp. 293–317.

Park, S.-J. (1985) 'Informalismus als Managementrationalität', in S.-J. Park (ed.), *Japanisches Management in der Praxis. Flexibilität oder Kontrolle im Prozess der Internationalisierung und Mikroelektronisierung* (Berlin: Express Edition), pp. 101–18.

Porter, M., H. Takeuchi and M. Sakakibara (2000) *Can Japan Compete?* (London: Macmillan).

Pucik, V. (1999) 'Where Performance Does not Matter: Human Resource Management in Japanese-Owned US Affiliates', in S. Beechler and A. Bird (eds), *Japanese Multinationals Abroad: Individual and Organizational Learning* (Oxford: Oxford University Press), pp. 169–88.

Pudelko, M. (2000): *Das Personalmanagement in Deutschland, den USA und Japan. Vol. 1: Die gesamtgesellschaftlichen Rahmenbedingungen im Wettbewerb der Systeme; Vol. 2: Eine systematische und vergleichende Bestandsaufnahme; Vol. 3: Wie wir voneinander lernen können* (Cologne: Saborowski).

Pudelko, M. (2004a) 'HRM in Japan and the West: What are the Lessons to Be Learnt from Each Other?', *Asian Business and Management*, 3, pp. 337–61.

Pudelko, M. (2004b) 'Benchmarking: Was amerikanische, japanische und deutsche Personalmanager voneinander lernen', *Zeitschrift für Personalforschung*, 18 (2), pp. 139–63.

Pudelko, M. (2005) 'Japanese Human Resource Management: From Being a Miracle to Needing One', in R. Haak and M. Pudelko (eds), *Japanese Management: the Search for a New Balance Between Continuity and Change* (Basingstoke and New York: Palgrave).

Rehfeld, J. E. (1995) *Das Beste aus Fernost und West. Management perfekt kombinieren* (Landsberg/Lech: Verlag Moderne Industrie).

Reinhold, G. (1992) *Wirtschaftsmanagement und Kultur in Ostasien. Sozial-kulturelle Determinanten wirtschaftlichen Handelns in China und Japan* (Munich: Iudicium).

Sommer, T. (1998) 'Der Irrtum der Propheten', *Die Zeit*, 2 January, p. 1.

Sullivan, J. J. (1992) 'Japanese Management Philosophies: From the Vacuous to the Brilliant', *California Management Review*, 34 (2), pp. 66–87.

Tayeb, M. (1995) 'The Competitive Advantage of Nations: The Role of HRM and Its Socio-Cultural Context', *International Journal for Human Resource Management*, 6 (3), pp. 588–605.

Teramoto, Y. and C. Benton (2005) 'Organizational Learning Mechanisms for Corporate Revitalization', in R. Haak and M. Pudelko (eds), *Japanese Management: The Search for a New Balance Between Continuity and Change* (Basingstoke and New York: Palgrave).

Westney, D. E. (1999) 'Changing Perspectives on the Organization of Japanese Multinational Companies', in S. Beechler and A. Bird (eds), *Japanese Multinationals Abroad: Individual and Organizational Learning* (Oxford: Oxford University Press), pp. 11–29.

Woronoff, J. (1992) *The Japanese Management Mystique. The Reality Behind the Myth* (Chicago and Cambridge: Irwin).

7
Employment Deregulation and the Expanding Market for Temporary Labour in Japan

Jun Imai and Karen Shire

Since the late 1990s labour market deregulation has increased the importance of the external labour market as a source of skilled labour and flexible employment in Japan. This has mainly happened through the legalization and diffusion of temporary employment, both in the form of fixed-term contracts (*keiyaku*) and various types of temporary agency employment (*haken*, called dispatched employment in Japanese translations into English). The traditional measures used to achieve employment flexibility in the internal (and firm-group) labour market, such as the short-term dispatching of skilled workers (*shukkô*), the permanent transfer of older and redundant workers (*tenseki*) or their reemployment under different (and lesser) contract terms (*shokutaku*) reached their limit in the low-growth era of the 1990s when firms had to reduce their workforces and restructure their personnel practices in order to redress serious mismatches between the internal labour supply and their demand for labour (Inagami, 1989, 2003; Nagai, 1997; Kumazawa, 1997; Hyôdô, 1997). Internal labour mobility has characterized human resource management in the case of core employees – those employed directly by firms under regular employment conditions, which in Japan typically involves an implicit long-term (or non-fixed) employment contract. Two of the most common forms of using external workers – part-time employment (*paato, arubaito*) and the short-term co-option of workers from supplier companies (*kônai ukeoi*) (Sato, 2001) – in the past were utilized for jobs requiring lower skills and were thus deemed unsuitable for expanding industries where knowledge-intensive work related to information and communication technology and high-value-added services had come into demand.

Temporary employment in Japan has also been limited by state regulations that either prevented (in the case of temporary agency work) or restricted (in the case of fixed-term contract workers) the market for non-regular employment. The tight regulation of temporary employment persisted well into the late 1990s. Nonetheless the growing practice of outsourcing to subcontractors (*kônai ukeoi*) and the entry of Manpower, the US multinational temporary employment agency, into Japan in 1962 meant that the triangular employment relation[1] typical of temporary agency work began to spread after the oil shocks in the 1970s, despite the formal legal barriers.

By the early 1990s, before the low-growth era, the demand for flexible employment grew for new and skilled lines of work connected with technological change and internationalization, and measures were taken to legalize temporary employment in order to create at least a small supply of labour to meet this demand. Change accelerated between 1990 and 2003, when successive revisions of state regulations opened the external labour market as a source of skilled and flexible labour. These revisions removed most of the restrictions on temporary agency and contract work and legalized private employment agencies, leading to the expansion of the private personnel placement sector and thus the supply of temporary workers.[2] The following analysis will show that the relationship between the internal and external labour markets as sources of skilled and experienced labour in Japan is shifting as firms continue to reduce their core workforces and rely more on temporary labour.

Deregulation of the market for temporary labour in Japan

In the 1990s major changes were made to the regulation of Japanese employment. These changes involved the lifting of three sets of limitations on temporary employment, regulated by three post-World War II employment laws: the limitations on fixed-term contracts set by the 1947 Labor Standards Act (*Rôdô kijun-hô*), the limitations on the operation and coverage of private job placement services under the 1947 Employment Security Law (*Shokugyô antei-hô*), and the restrictions on temporary agency work laid out in the 1986 Temporary Dispatched Work Law (*Rôdôsha haken-hô*), which first legalized the temporary employment sector (Table 7.1). The years 1999 and 2003 brought the most radical changes to the regulations in terms of deregulating temporary work and the operation of private firms engaged in personnel placement.

Temporary agency work has received the most attention in the deregulation effort, with five major changes since the legalization of this type of

80

Table 7.1   Changes in the labour supply and temporary work regulations, 1986–2003

1986	Temporary Dispatched Work Law: legalization of the use of temporary agency workers in 13 designated occupations (called the 'positive list').
1990	Revision of the Temporary Dispatched Work Law: extension of the positive list of occupations from 13 to 16; extension of the term of temporary employment from nine months to one year.
1994	Revision of the Temporary Dispatched Work Law: for older workers (aged 60 and over), replacement of the positive list with a short negative list of occupations, prohibiting temporary employment in only a few occupations.
1996	Revision of the Temporary Dispatching Work Law: extension of the positive list from 16 to 26.
1997	Revision of the Employment Security Law: under the 1947 law, private placement had only been allowed for jobs on the positive list of occupations, the revision replaced the positive list with a negative list, and relaxed the limitations on fees and the regulations on the establishment of private personnel placement firms.
1999	Revision of the Labour Standards Act: fixed-term contracts, which had been limited to short-term, project-related work and limited to one-year since 1947, were declared legal for most forms of professional and knowledge-intensive work, and the permitted duration was increased to three years.
1999	Revision of the Temporary Dispatched Work Law: this revision of the 1987 law replaced the positive list with a negative list, set a one year limit on temporary employment in newly allowable occupations, and extended the term to three years for the 26 occupations allowed under the 1996 revision to the law.
1999	Revision of the Employment Security Law: removed all but two[1] occupations on the negative list.
2003	Revision of the Labour Standards Act: The duration of fixed-term contracts for all project-related work was extended to three years; for professional and knowledge-intensive work the limit was extended to five years.
2003	Revision of the Temporary Dispatched Work Law: partial removal of the negative list system and extension of the term of temporary employment to three years for all occupations except those in manufacturing.
2003	Revision of the Employment Security Law: loosening of the conditions on starting a private personnel placement firm, placement limitations lifted for jobs in selected service industries such as restaurants and hotels.

Note:
1. Note that in these industries other loose regulations permit a great deal of flexibility. These are also industries where day labourers have been concentrated (Gill, 2001).

Source: Imai (2004).

employment in 1986. From that time female temps undertaking clerical work accounted for about 80 per cent of all agency workers, though a number of new and highly skilled occupations dominated by men were also opened to temporary agency workers. Temporary agency work was limited to a list of specific occupations. The first major change to the law in 1994 encouraged the creation of a market for older male temporary workers, and by the late 1990s temporary agencies were a well-established source of peripheral employees (non-core female employees and older male employees who had once been core workers). Large firms in particular seized upon the chance to externalize whole segments of female clerical work by using temporary agencies. A major car manufacturer, for example, established its own temporary agency in the early 1990s and thereafter sourced most of its young female recruits from that agency (Shire, 1999). An important new development was the establishment of temporary agencies for professional and technical workers (mainly male) in the new media, information and communication industries, where there was often a mismatch between the supply of and demand for such workers.

The aim of the deregulations in 1999 and 2003 was to expand the market for skilled male temporary workers. The 1994 reform did so for older men aged 60 and over, and the 1999 deregulation lifted most of the occupational restrictions, thus permitting the use of temporary agency workers in most of the labour market. The expansion of male temporary employment was also closely linked to the deregulation of fixed-term contract work in the late 1990s. Some forms of temporary contract had always been permitted under the Japanese Labour Standards Act, but changes in 1999 and 2003 legalized the use of fixed-term contracts for professional and highly skilled knowledge workers. The time restrictions on the length of fixed-term contracts were also relaxed, first from one year to three and then to five years for skilled workers.

Two developments in the deregulation process contributed significantly to the opening of the market for temporary labour: changes in the stance of the Ministry of Labour on the use of the external labour market to solve the two main employment problems of the 1990s – demand and supply mismatches and unemployment; and the growing part played by the special Cabinet Committee on Deregulation in deliberating upon and drafting revisions to employment regulations (Imai, 2004). In a 1999 white paper the ministry explained its changing attitude towards employment security. For the first time, the Ministry expressed doubt about the ability of traditional internal labour mobility practices to curb unemployment. Moreover it admitted that employment security in the form of lifetime employment may even have prevented firms from adapting to external economic changes (Ministry of Labour, 1999). It therefore stressed the importance of reorganizing the external labour market to solve the problem. Among specific measures to improve the employability of workers, it suggested that the labour markets for *paato* (female part-time employees) and temporary agency workers (*haken*) could be improved by closer cooperation between public placement agencies and private personnel placement firms (ibid.).

The revisions of the Temporary Dispatched Work Law in the 1990s also reflected the ministry's changed position on the external labour market. Under the revision of 1994 temporary work was permitted in almost all occupations for workers aged 60 years or older. This measure was expected to remedy the poor employment opportunities for older workers, especially after retirement. A further revision in 1996 expanded the list of permitted occupations in order to solve employment mismatches, which had resulted in a tight labour market for highly skilled workers. The results of the radical revisions of the Temporary Dispatched Work and the Employment Security Laws – the liberalization of temporary agency employment and removal of the public monopoly on job placement services – were considered a turning point in the history of Japanese labour market policy (Suwa, 2000, p. 9)[3] and a clear step towards the creation of an industry for private staff placement and personnel services (Tsuchida, 2000).

While the revisions of the Temporary Dispatched Work Law were usually discussed by a Ministry of Labour advisory committee (*shingikai*) with trade union participation, the plans for the 1997 revision were begun not by the ministry but by a cabinet deregulation committee (Takanashi, 2001). In 1994 the Murayama government established the Administrative Reform Committee (*Gyôsei kaikaku iinkai*) – headed by Iida Yôtarô, chairman of Mitsubishi Heavy Industries – to discuss the reform of government agencies and deregulation. Under the Administrative Reform Committee, a Special Committee on Deregulation (*Kisei kanwa shô iinkai*) was set up. This was headed by Miyauchi Yoshihiko, chairman of ORIX Corporation. Unions were only occasionally represented in these committees and the dominant influence of employers was clear. In 1995 and 1996 the Special Committee on Deregulation published a series of deregulation proposals, and these influenced the discussions on reform by the Ministry of Labour advisory committees (*shingikai*) (Takanashi, 2001; Miura, 2001a), which previously had set their own agendas. The strengthened role of employers in the policy-making process and the weakening of that of unions enabled the expansion of temporary employment, from an employment form restricted to special cases and skilled female workers, to domains of work where core male employees might be replaced by temporary workers.

The Expansion of the market for temporary labour

The deregulation of temporary employment has fuelled the expansion of the temporary help industry in the past few years, in terms not only of the number of firms and temporary workers but also of the range of services offered by temporary help firms. From the point of view of client companies, the temporary help industry offers a means of expanding the external non-core workforce and outsourcing two aspects of the traditional Japanese personnel management function – the recruitment of white-collar clerical workers and the placement of redundant older workers. In essence the firms in the sector are transforming themselves into personnel service providers. For female (whether young temporary workers or older part-time ones) and older workers the external labour market has become the main means of employment, while for male workers the expansion of temporary work constitutes a significant diversification of their employment prospects as there is a growing likelihood that at some point in their working lives they will be part of the external labour market, which in Japan is becoming a euphemism for being in a non-regular form of employment. This section looks at the expansion of temporary employment, temporary help firms and the temporary help business.

Temporary employees

Part-time employment is still the largest category of non-regular (*hiseishain*) work in Japan, but since the 1998/99 deregulations the expansion of temporary employment has proceeded at a much greater pace. Table 7.2 and the analysis that follows are based on the Employment Status Survey, which is conducted every five years.[4]

Between 1987 and 1992, during the peak of the bubble economy, total employment rose from 46,153,000 to 52,575,000. During that time the number of regular employees (including executives) increased by 4.4 million, compared with 1.9 million for non-regular employees. Between 1992 and 1997 there was an overall employment increase of 2.4 million, but for the first time this was mainly due to the expansion of non-regular employment. Between the 1997 and 2002 surveys, regular employees fell dramatically by 4.4 million, but in terms of the proportion of total employment, regular work contracts still accounted from 70 per cent of the total in 2002. At the same time, non-regular employment increased by 3.6 million to reach 30 per cent of all employees. Because overall employment did not change much in this period, non-regular employment is gradually replacing regular employment contracts.[5]

In 2002 part-time work accounted for 22 per cent of total employment in Japan, and although the number of temporary dispatched (agency)

Table 7.2 Number of employees by type of employment, 1987–2002 (thousands, percentages in brackets)

	1987		1992		1997		2002	
Regular employees	34,565	(74.9)	38,062	(72.4)	38,542	(70.1)	34,557	(63.1)
Executives	3,088	(6.7)	3,970	(7.6)	3,850	(7.0)	3,895	(7.1)
Non-regular employees	8,497[1]	(18.4)	10,532	(20.0)	12,590	(23.0)	16,206	(29.6)
Part-time (paato, arubaito)	6,563	(14.2)	8,481	(16.1)	10,342	(18.8)	12,062	(22.0)
Agency (haken)	87	(0.2)	163	(0.3)	257	(0.5)	721	(1.3)
Fixed-term contract (keiyaku shlokutaku	730	(1.6)	880	(1.7)	966	(1.8)	2,477	(4.5)
Other	1,118	(2.4)	1,008	(1.9)	1,025	(1.9)	946	(1.7)
Total[2]	46,153	(100.0)	52,575	(100.0)	54,997	(100.0)	54,733	(100.0)

Notes:
1. Total lower due to rounding.
2. Total higher due to missing answers in reports of specific employment.

Source: Shūgyō-kōzō kihon chōsa (Employment Status Surveys).

workers had grown rapidly they still only amounted to 1.3 per cent of the total in 2002. In terms of numbers, the most substantial increase was in the number of fixed-term contract workers, whose share of total employment rose from 1.8 per cent in 1997 to 4.5 per cent in 2002. The expansion of fixed-term contract work was closely related to the development of the temporary help industry in general. While temporary work continued to be dominated by females, since the deregulations took effect in 1999, the number of male temporary workers has risen considerably especially in manufacturing occupations. The number of fixed-term contract workers more than doubled in the transport/communication, manufacturing and technical/professional work, all of which are core domains of the Japanese employment system (Imai, 2004).

The development of the temporary employment sector

In terms of the number of enterprises, their financial turnover and the services they offer, the temporary help industry has grown tremendously since the deregulations of the late 1990s. In 2002 there were an estimated 14,655 temporary help enterprises, 60 per cent more than in 1997.[6] Annual turnover doubled between 1997 and 2002 to more than 22 billion.

The demand for temporary workers has grown almost evenly in medium-sized and large firms, the strongest increase being in the use of fixed-term contract workers. The use of part-time workers is more

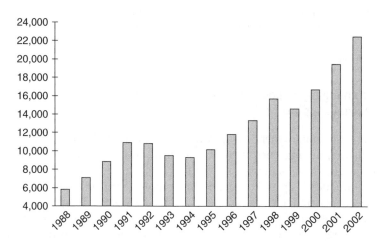

Source: Rôdôsha haken jigyô jigyô hôkoku (business report by the help industry).

Figure 7.1   Annual turnover in the temporary help industry, 1988–2002 (billion yen)

common among smaller firms (Imai, 2004). According to the most recent Employment Status Survey, the proportion of regular employees in large companies – the best measure of the maintenance of lifetime employment in the Japanese human resource management system – declined from 89 per cent in 1987 to 74 per cent in 2002, with an accompanying increase in non-regular employees. The greatest increase has been in the number of temporary workers (both agency and fixed-contract), who together account for more than 8 per cent of total employees in large companies.

Since the deregulations the types of industry using temporary workers have expanded from finance and insurance to ICT and other high-value-added service industries (ibid.) and temporary help firms have increased their range of services. The latter now include the provision of temporary workers, business services conducted by agency employees, job recruitment, the placement of fixed-term contract workers and the placement of redundant workers. The last of these seems to be unique to Japan and is tied to the recent practice by large firms of shedding their older workers. Under the general heading of *jinzai bijinesu* (personnel services business), temporary help firms take on entire groups of older workers who in earlier times would have been transferred (*tenseki suru*) to allied or subsidiary firms within the firm's group (*keiretsu*). In 2002 the largest Japanese temporary help firm – Pasona, which calls this new product 'restructuring services' (*risutora shien jigyô*) – reported that almost a third of its profits derived from this business (Pasona Inc., 2003). Thus, Japanese companies are turning to the external labour market not only for flexible employment, but also to overcome the problem of redundant (especially older) employees.

The changing balance between internal and external supplies of skilled labour

Temporary employment has grown in all occupational groups, across all industries, among both men and women, and in all sizes of firm in Japan. The deregulations since the late 1990s have opened the market for temporary help and created both a supply of and a demand for out-sourced personnel services covering skilled workers. Temporary help firms supply both agency employees and contract workers, and are in the process of expanding their services to include the recruitment, training and reemployment of skilled workers.

Government deregulation has opened the market for temporary labour, but firms engaged in placing temporary workers are organizing the supply and creating further demand for skilled and flexible workers. The changing balance between regular and non-regular employees (see Table 7.2 above) is a rough indicator of the changing balance between the external labour market and internal labour mobility and lifetime employment in firms. Growth in the temporary employment of white-collar workers is a more precise indicator of the rising importance of the external labour market for the supply of skilled and flexible workers. The steady flow of computer operators, technical and professional workers and the expanding number of sales and service workers into temporary employment mean that the external workforce can now be characterized as a skilled workforce, with a strategic role in areas of work transformed by new technology and internationalization.

Since 1999 the use of temporary workers has been permitted in more manufacturing occupations, and the latter now account for 27 per cent of all agency and 25 per cent of all fixed-contract employees. The extension of temporary employment into manufacturing, once the bastion of union power and job protection in Japan, was the result of the prominent part played by employers (and the near absence of labour representation) in the deregulation committees and the changing attitude of the Ministry of Labour towards the protection of employment in the face of internal labour market failures.

A relatively undiscussed aspect of the expansion of temporary labour is the part played by the temporary help industry itself. The emerging external labour market for skilled labour in Japan is increasingly being organized by temporary help firms. Even fixed-term contract workers, who elsewhere make up the ranks of the new self-employed, often have temporary help firms as employers. Finally some aspects of human resource management at Japanese firms are being handled by temporary agencies. Because there is a middleman in the picture – the temporary help/personnel services firm – it is not correct to interpret the expansion of temporary work in Japan as the expansion of market-driven employment, as scholars have done in the case of the United States (Cappelli, 1999). Relying on suppliers for labour, and on inter-firm relations for labour exchanges, remains a part of the story of achieving mobility and flexibility in Japanese human resource management. Increasingly however, the suppliers belong to a new and rapidly growing industry, of private (and largely independent) personnel service firms.

Notes

1. 'Triangular employment relation' refers to the contract between the temporary work agency, the temporary worker and the client firm. While the employer is typically considered to be the temporary employment agency, the employee works at and is under the authority of the client company.
2. The regulations restricted both the use of temporary employees to certain jobs and the operations of firms that placed these employees. Until the complete deregulation of private personnel placement services in 1999, firms engaged in the placement of agency temps and other workers were limited to specific occupations and employment situations.
3. Suwa had been chairperson of the Special Committee on Private Job Placement, which was created under the Advisory Committee (*shingikai*) on Employment Security at the Ministry of Labour, and was responsible for leading the government committees involved in the revisions of the Temporary Dispatched Work Law in 1994, 1996 and 1999.
4. The Employment Status Survey (*Shûgyô-kôzô kihon chôsa*) is conducted every five years by the Japanese Statistics Bureau. The sampling procedure is based on the national microcensus. The 1997 survey was conducted in 29,000 microregions and included about 430,000 households and approximately 1,100,000 individuals. The results are considered to be representative of the entire Japanese population. The categorization of non-regular employment relies on statements by the respondents.
5. The absence of longitudinal panel surveys prohibits a clear analysis of replacement effects at the level of individual employment biographies.
6. We have not been able to find a reliable source for the number of temporary help firms in Japan. Figures presented here are based on a business report by the temporary help industry.

References

Cappelli, P. (1999) *The New Deal at Work: Managing the Market-Driven Workforce.* (Cambridge, Mass.: Harvard Business School Press).

Gill, T. (2001) *Men of Uncertainty: The social organisation of day laborers in contemporary Japan* (Albany, NY: Suny Press).

Hyôdô, T. (1997) *Rôdô no sengo-shi* (The postwar history of labour relations) (Tokyo: University of Tokyo Press).

Imai, J. (2004) *The Rise of Temporary Employment in Japan: Legalisation and Expansion of a Non-Regular Employment Form*, discussion paper (Duisburg: Institute of East Asian Studies, Duisburg-Essen University).

Inagami, T. (1989) *Tenkan-ki no rôdô sekai* (The world of work in transition) (Tokyo: Yûshin-dô).

Inagami, T. (2003) *Kigyô gurûpu keiei to shukkô tenseki kankô* (Corporate group management and the practice of *shukkô* and *tenseki*) (Tokyo: University of Tokyo Press).

Kumazawa, M. (1997) *Nôryoku-shugi to kigyô shakai* (Performance orientation and corporate society) (Tokyo: Iwanami Shoten).

Ministry of Labour (ed.) (1999) *Rôdô hakushô: kyûsoku ni henka suru rôdô shijô to aratana koyô no sôshutsu* (White Paper on Labour: The rapidly changing labour market and the creation of new employment opportunities). (Tokyo: Japan Institute of Labour).

Miura, M. (2001a) 'Daihyô-sei, setsumei sekinin, seisaku yukô-sei, haken-hô no seisaku keisei katei wo seisaku hyôka suru ichi shiron' (Representation, accountability and policy effectiveness: evaluating the policy-making process for the 1999 revision of the Temporary Dispatch Law), *The Monthly Journal of the Japan Institute of Labour* (497) (January), pp. 33–43.

Miura, M. (2001b) 'Rengô no seisaku sanka: rôki-hô/haken-hô wo chûshin ni' (Rengô's participation in policy making: the cases of the revision of the Labour Standards Act and the Temporary Dispatch Law), in K. Nakamura (ed.), *Rôdô kumiai no mirai wo saguru*, (Searching for the Future of Labour Unions) (Tokyo: Rengô Sôgô Sekikatsu Kaihatsu Kenkyû-jo), pp. 498–559.

Nagai, Y. (1997) 'Koyô rôdô shijô no danryoku-ka senryaku to nihon-teki rôshi kankei: haken rôdô no katsuyô jittai to sono henka wo fumaete' (Flexible employment strategies and Japanese style labor relations: the use of temporary dispatch workers under change), in *Tenkanki no kigyô shakai* (Corporate Society in Transition), *Nihon rôdô shakai-gakkai nenpô* (*Annals of the Japanese Association of Labour Sociology*) (Tokyo: Tôshin-dô), pp. 37–63.

Pasona Inc. (2003) *2002 nen 5 gatsu-ki chûkan kessan setsumeikai* (Pasona Business Report 2002) (Tokyo: Pasona).

Sato, H. (2001) 'Atarashii jinzai katsuyô senryaku no genjô to rôdô kumiai no taiô' (New human resource strategies and the Responses of trade unions) in (Electronic Workers Union) and H. Sato (ed.), *IT jidai no koyô shisutemu* (The IT-Era Employment System) (Tokyo: Nihon hyôron sha), pp. 7–37.

Shire, K. (1999) 'Gendered Organisation and Workplace Culture in Japanese Customer Services', *Social Science Journal Japan*, 3 (1), pp. 37–57.

Suwa, Y. (2000) 'Rôdô shijô-hô no rinen to taikei' (Labour market law: idea and system), in *Nihon Rôdô-hô Gakkai* (Japanese Association of Labour Law) (ed.), *Kôza 21seiki no rôdô-hô dai 2 kan rôdô shijô no kikou to ruru* (Labour Law in the 21st Century. Volume 2: The System and the Regulation of the Labour Market), (Tokyo: Yûhikaku), pp. 2–22.

Takanashi, A. (2000) 'Rôdô seisaku no ritsuan katei' (The formation of labour policy) *The Monthly Journal of the Japan Institute of Labour*, (475) (January), p. 1.

Takanashi, A. (2001) 'Dai 2-han shôkai rôdôsha haken-hô' (Second version of the Temporary Dispatch Work Law) (Tokyo: Japan Institute of Labour).

Tsuchida, M. (2000) 'Kaisei shokugyô antei-hô no igi to kadai' (The meaning and future agenda of the revised employment security law), *The Monthly Journal of the Japan Institute of Labour*, (475) (January), pp. 36–47.

8
Employment Practices in Japanese Firms: Can *Mikoshi* Management Survive?

David Methé and Junichiro Miyabe

Introduction

The *Hakata Gion* festival has been held every year in mid-July in the city of Fukuoka on the island of Kyushu since some time in the Heian period (794–900). It begins on 1 July and ends on 15 July with the *Oiyama* race, in which seven teams each carry a *Yamagasa Mikoshi* – a one-ton float – around a set course. At 4.59 am the seven floats, representing various civic or business groups in Fukuoka and carried on the shoulders of 26 men, sequentially depart from the *Kushida* Shrine. After a short timed race at the start of the course, which requires a sprint from a starting line around a pole and back to the line the race takes to the streets. During this five kilometre section the carriers of the *Yamagasa Mikoshi* are replaced by others. More than 100 men run alongside or behind the float and it is from their ranks that the successive replacements are drawn. Several men sit on top of the *Yamagasa Mikosh* and shout encouragement to the bearers below.

In this chapter we describe a stereotypical image of the Japanese management system that we term *Mikoshi* management. Like the large *Yamagasa Mikoshi* carried during the *Hakata Gion* festival, management systems in Japan can be viewed as an organization supported by the pillars of the Japanese management system (JMS) and include *Shusin koyo* (lifetime employment system), *nenko jorestu* (seniority based salary system), the enterprise unions, stable shareholding, cross-shareholding and main banks (for a discussion of these pillars see Methé, 2005). The *Mikoshi* encapsulates the company as an economic community of stakeholders and forms the basis of the many human resource practices that exist within the organization, as well as determining the working of the latter and the identity of the people carrying it. The various pillars of the management system support these practices, but it is the actions of the employees that make the organization move and adapt to changes in the environment.

The title of this chapter refers to the challenges that this system of management has confronted over the past decade and will confront in even stronger forms over the next decade: the ageing of the population and the decline in the birth rate, resulting in a decreasing number of young workers and a growing number of older workers. This raises the question of what role the older workers can play. Currently the retirement age is 60, while the average life expectancy is 78.36 years for men and 85.33 years for women (Ministry Health Welfare and Labour, 2003a). What do people do in the years after retirement? The increasing trend towards part-time work, as exhibited by the existence of NEET (people who are not in employment, education, or training) phenomenon, which may partially be the results of attemps at the preservation of the *nenko joretsu* and *shushin koyo* systems (Methé, 2005), certainly presents long-term challenges to these systems and to Japanese society. Whether by choice or circumstance, a growing proportion of young people are not joining the ranks of regular employees, so how can they develop productive skills and contribute to the economy and society over their lifetime? The trend among those who do enter and stay within the ranks of regular employees is to want greater control over their careers and not have them determined by the whims or plans of the *jinjibu* (personnel department). This has caused concern in Japanese companies about the fate of their identity as economic community, especially as they are confronting the need to engage in mid-career recruitment and are starting to rely on part-time, non-regular workers to carry out more of the firm's core activities.

Women are playing a greater part in the workforce as regular or part-time employees, posing a challenge to the usually all-male ranks at the upper end of the management hierarchy. As the overall workforce shrinks, the importance of women as a source of productive and creative labour will increase proportionally.

Mikoshi management

We start with the people who sit on top of the *Mikoshi* and shout encouragement to those carrying it. In our analogy these are the executive managers of large Japanese organizations. They are not beholden to outside shareholders, and with the weakening of the main bank system they have become omnipotent in the company. The only disciplinary mechanisms are external: the product market and governmental regulations and laws.

In order to understand the process of change in large Japanese companies it is necessary to consider some of the dynamics involved in choosing senior executives. The incumbent president of the company usually chooses his successor and then takes the post of chairman. Therefore he does not leave, but he is less involved in the day-to-day running of the company. Meanwhile the new president has yet to establish his power base so is dependent on the power base of the previous president to get anything done. Those who occupy the presidential seat are more than caretakers but less than the remakers of the system that the presidents of US companies are.

The succession process usually starts with the current president (*shacho*) asking the current *kaicho* (chairman) to step aside. The current *shacho*, or someone with his support, such as a senior vice president – will then occupy the *kaicho's* seat. The outgoing *kaicho* is often asked to remain as an executive advisor (*sodan yaku*) or *komon* (consoler). Japanese leaders are not active agents of change or people who put their imprint on the company; rather they wait for middle managers to come to them with proposals and then act as facilitators and coordinators of the implemention of these proposals (Nonaka, 1988). Thus leaders push within the group as opposed to pulling the group in a particular direction (Ballon and Honda, 2000). We shall return to this subject later.

In the late 1980s and early 1990s the position of executive advisor (*sodan yaku*) was gradually being eliminated, especially in the banking industry. Doubt was raised about the value of these advisors, particularly as non-performing loans had been generated during their tenure. In addition some companies, including Sony and Orix, moved towards a more US style of governance, with committees determining the composition and remuneration of the board and senior management.

Irrespective of the form of governance, however, the role of leaders has not noticeably changed. This is not to say that leaders who shape and direct their companies do not exist. Inaba of Fanuc and Inamori of Kyocera are such leaders, as was Honda Soichiro of Honda Motors and Morita of Sony. Small and medium-sized companies often have such leaders, if for no other reason than they have to have someone at the helm of the company. That person may be the founder or the founder's son. These leaders take risks and sometimes fail, but the alternative to not taking the risk of moving the company forward is to watch it slowly fail.

As noted earlier, executive managers hold considerable governance power in large companies as there is little involvement of capital markets and investment institutions. In the absence of financial market discipline of management, traditionally the main bank system has been the primary external governance source (Aoki and Patrick, 1994). In recent years, however, the position of the main bank has weakened in this regard. The number of companies in which the five major banking groups – Resona, UFJ, Mizuho, Tokyo Mitsubishi and Mitsui Sumitomo – are among the top ten shareholders has declined over the past two years.[1] As this equity position has been the primary source of power in the main bank system, the more that banks sell off their equity in companies the more the main bank system will weaken. Survey evidence also suggests that companies intend to rely less on their main bank as a source of funding.

Accompanying this trend has been the continuing consolidation of the banking sector, and the proposed merger between UFJ and Tokyo Mitsubishi will further reduce competition in the sector. In any event it is difficult to see the main bank system reasserting itself. It may take a new form, but what this might be remains to be seen. In recent years pension funds and other large institutional investors have begun to take more interest in governance. For example at shareholders' meetings they have begun to question managers and to vote against management-proposed initiatives. Nonetheless the assertion of minority shareholder rights and the possibility of hostile takeovers and other features of the US system are not yet evident in Japan.[2]

Because of the weakening of the main bank system and the relative lack of participation by equity holders, Japanese companies are in the interesting position of being capitalist companies without strong capitalist leadership. Managers run the companies but these managers are essentially faceless to most of Japanese society, let alone the rest of the world. Only when a company becomes embroiled in a scandal (Mitsubishi Motors is a recent example) or loses market share and profits (for example Sony) do the faces of senior managers appear. Even the heads of successful companies such as Toyota, Honda, Canon, Sharp, Rohm, and Nidec rarely seek or are granted the publicity given to their Western counterparts. Few take the path of writing books extolling the management principles that have enabled their companies to weather the storms that have buffeted the Japanese economy. In essence this capitalist system – run not by capitalists but by all-powerful managers who are constrained by routines and rituals and are relatively faceless – determines the employment practices that make up what we term *Mikoshi* management.

In a survey of CEOs of Japanese, Korean and Chinese companies, a significant percentage of the Korean and Chinese CEO's stated that the quality of top management was the key to competitive advantage (43 per cent and 46 per cent respectively) but few Japanese managers agreed (13.2 per cent). Instead the latter felt that competitive advantage depended largely on the activities of employees in the workplace (*Nihon Keizai Shimbun*, 24 March 2004). Leadership is not exerted by people outside the work group, as in the West, but from within the group (Ballon and Honda, 2000).

Although Japanese business leaders occupy positions of formal authority they have risen up through and been socialized into the ranks of employees of the company. This begins soon after recruitment. Larger companies often ask recently hired employees to return to their old university to ask graduands to apply to the company. Those who are selected have an informal mentor in the form of the person who recruited them, to whom they can turn for information on appropriate ways to behave in the company. Each recruit is also assigned an official instructor, usually someone who has been working with the company for about five years, and this person is responsible for the recruit's on-the-job training during the first year. This is often called *te tori ashi tori*, or controlling both the hands and the feet of the person; that is, the instructor supervises the trainee's every movement. This creates a very special relationship between junior and more senior people. The old school tie also comes into play at a higher level, in that many schools and universities have alumni gatherings where very junior members of a company have the opportunity to meet and talk to very senior members. These social gatherings bind superior and subordinate together and open informal channels of communication.

In summary, at the core of the Japanese management system is the idea of the organization as an economic community composed of various stakeholders, with the employees being the key stakeholders and the primary *raison d'être* for the existence of the organization. In terms of *Mikoshi* management, senior managers move up through the ranks of regular employees in the lifetime employment system and are socialized into the particular organizational culture of the company they joined immediately after graduating. Managers devote considerable time to the market position of the company. The maximization of shareholder wealth is not the ultimate goal; rather it is to make sufficient profits to maintain the health of the company. Outside influences are minimal and are generally only brought to bear if the company falls into serious financial trouble or becomes involved in a scandal.

Change in the Japanese Management system and the issue of convergence

Systems survive by adapting to changes in their environment. As the variety of elements in the environment increases, systems must adjust to them or face being overwhelmed by that variety and succumbing to it (Ashby, 1952). When a system is complex and composed of many interacting levels (Morel and Ramanujam, 1999), change can occur at any level of the system (Gersick, 1991). Japanese management is a nested system of a complex system composed of various interconnecting layers. Change ranges from first-order or single loop changes that preserve the system in a homeostatic way, to second-order or double-loop changes that fundamentally alter the system (Argyris, 1976, 1992; Methé, 2005). However, in a complex system, a second-order change at one level of the system can also preserve the system at a higher level, making the consequences of the lower-level change first-order at the higher level. Convergence, as a form of change, can also occur at many levels. Here we shall focus on the overall governance of Japanese companies and the HRM aspects of the Japanese management system, and how these two elements feed back and feed forward into the core aspect of *Mikoshi* management: the idea of the company as an economic community of stakeholders.

Convergence usually refers to movement towards something. The 'something' of importance to many who study the Japanese system is the Western, especially the US management model, whose purpose is to maximize shareholders' wealth rather than serve the interests of those who make up the economic community of the company (Dunphy, 1987). It is argued here that the changes taking place in the traditional Japanese model may not imply that the latter is moving towards the Western model, but rather that is evolving in its own way in response to its own environmental influences.

The evolution of the Japanese management model

In 1950s and 1960s the developed economies were all moving in the same direction, with the United States at the apex. In the 1970s the question was raised as to whether Japan was similarly converging or was developing its own unique model, and in the 1980s it was even suggested that the new Japanese model might surpass or replace the US model.

The focus shifted again in the 1990s, when the Japanese economy encountered severe difficulties and the usual methods of addressing these did not work. The economy became mired in slow growth and deflation, and the country's large companies lost their seemingly unassailable global position. According to some, Japan had entered a lost decade (Yoshikawa, 2001), it had become arthritic and unable to change in a meaningful way (Lincoln, 2001) and its system had soured (Katz, 1998) because it could no longer deliver economic benefits to its constituents. It was only a matter of time before the Japanese economy and Japanese business would adopt the global standard (essentially the Anglo-American model) of economic and management practices. This view took firmer hold in Japan and the United States with the rapid growth of NASDAQ and the IT/dotcom bubble in 1999–2000. Since the IT bubble burst in the United States there has been less talk about adopting the global standard, but concern about governance transparency, non-performing loans and similar issues remains, calling into question the viability of the traditional Japanese management approach.

One of the pillars of the Japanese management is lifetime employment. Although some have argued that lifetime employment has outlived its usefulness and is on its way out (Hirakubo, 1999), it still appears to be viable. That the practice has economic benefits for the firms that engage in it has been recognized since the earliest studies of the Japanese Management System (Cole, 1972a, 1972b). Also, surveys conducted by various Japanese government ministries indicate that most firms and employees of all ages still see the value of maintaining the practice (Ministry of Health, Labour and Welfare, 2003b; METI, 2003).

It is our view that this element of *Mikoshi* management is still basically intact and will continue for the foreseeable future. However it is important to recognize that the definition of who actually enjoys lifetime employment has always been vague and that the employees who make up the core group may shift over time (Methé, 2005). This is especially true at the younger and older ends of the age scale. In the 1990s numerous companies hired a smaller number of graduates and asked many of their oldest workers to take early retirement. This has resulted in a shrinkage of the core group of employees who are viewed as permanent.

One consequence of the reduction of lifetime workers is the growing trend of employing part-time male and female workers. The proportion of females working part-time rise from 32.9 per cent in 1987 to 41.4 per cent in 2002, while those in regular employment fell from 62.9 per cent to 45 per cent. The trend was similar for males, with the proportion of regular workers falling from 90.9 per cent to 75.9 per cent and a corresponding rise in temporary workers. (Ministry of Health, Labour and Welfare, 1987, 1992, 1997, 2002). In the context of *Mikoshi* management the question is how to maintain a permanent workforce as more and more people work part-time. Part of the answer lies with the company union.

Union involvement in employment practices now encompasses the growing number of temporary employees. For a long time, temporary employees had second-class status in Japanese companies. With the exception of *Ito Yokado* and a few others in the retail sector, such as

Daiei, most companies only used temporary workers when the workload was pushed beyond a peak. Daiei was the first company to put temporary workers into managerial positions, ranging from floor manager to deputy store manager (*Nikkei Ryutsu Shimbun*, 25 April 2002).[3] Similarly Ito Yokado uses a large number of temporary employees to do the same jobs as those done by regular employees, including management jobs.[4] Hence the company has had to adjust its remuneration and promotion systems to provide an equitable distribution of the rewards for years of temporary service. Many companies in other sectors of the economy are now employing temporary workers to carry out jobs once done by regular employees. As a result the unions are moving to represent these workers and are treating them as part of the core employee group. This has also spurred interest in performance-related pay and its relationship to length of service. Since many of these employees are female, women's hither to restricted role in companies may begin to change in terms of promotion opportunities and task assignments (Jones, 1976–77; Edwards, 1988; Royalty, 1996; Schein *et al.*, 1996; Appold *et al.*, 1998).

Another trend is that a growing number of younger people, both male and female, are concerned about building their careers. Just five years ago the concept of a personalized career was almost unheard of. In surveys conducted regularly by the Japan Productivity Centre, respondents recently recruited to firms are asked to name the factors that were most important in their decision to join the firm. In 1971, 27 per cent responded that the future prospects of the company was the most important factor and only 19 per cent mentioned the possibility of building a career. However in 2004 fewer than 10 per cent thought that the future prospects of the firm were important while over 30 per cent had joined their firm because it offered the opportunity of career building (*Nihon Keizai Shimbun*, 18 June 2004).

This change in attitude has led many large companies to introduce the concept of 'free agency', or a mobile internal labour market. This is different from the past practice in that jobs are not filled through regular rotation in the traditional way. Then employees' careers were determined by the personnel department and they stayed with the company throughout their working lives. Now many younger professional employees are aware and even state that they may not be staying with the company indefinitely and wish to acquire skills, knowledge and experience that will make them more marketable to other companies. Companies' response has been to attempt to maintain their core group of employees by enabling them to develop their careers within the company in the hope that they will stay. This is an example of

heterodynamic change at one level of the system-the fundamental altering of the HRM practice of job rotation in order to preserve a higher-
level element of the Japanese management system; that is, a core group
of employees who are loyal to the company.

Although many companies such as Isetan, Tohoku Denryoku,
Shiseido, Toshiba, NEC System, Asahi Kasei, Fujitsu, Epson, Keiyu, Isuzu,
Ishikawajima Harima Heavy Industry, Daiei, Dai Nippon Printing,
which represent a range of industries have instituted such 'free agency'
systems, we will look at one. The case of Toshiba is representative for the
new system. Under its system, regular employees with five years or more
experience with the company are eligible to enter the free agent system.
They can seek a transfer to a different section or department of their
choice without the consent of their immediate manager by applying
directly to the *jinjibu* (personnel department). However, the *jinjibu*
maintains the system. Those employees who wish to move to another
department will access the system and view what jobs are available and
then apply directly to the manager of that department. After an interview, if both the manager and the employee agree, the employee will
transfer to the new department, which will then inform the personnel
department that the change has taken place. About 40,000 Toshiba
employees are eligible for the system, but no figures are publicly available on the actual number of employees who have joined it (*Nikkei
Sangyo Shimbun*, 8 November, 2002).

Another issue is relevant to our discussion of changes to *Mikoshi* management is the introduction of merit-based pay systems. What is meant
by merit pay in the context of the existing *nenko joretsu* (seniority-based
wage system) has varied among scholars. Aoki (1990) noted that merit is
part of the traditional *nenko joretsu* system. Inohara (1990) and Sugimoto
(2003) claim that *nenko joretsu* takes into consideration a broader definition of merit than recognized in Western applications. This definition is
not tied to specific skills or task accomplishments per se, but to more
general capabilities that accumulate over time and with experience. The
attempt by Fujitsu and others to implement merit-based pay on the
basis of clearly defined objectives and the accomplishment of those
objectives is running into problems due to the lack of experience with
the merit-based pay system (*Nikkei Sangyo Shimbun*, 10 April, 2001, and
Nikkei Sangyo Shimbun, 18 May 2001; Methé, 2005). Some companies are
now reconsidering their experiments with the practice and some are
considering whether to drop it altogether.

The *nenko joretsu* system is moving away from pay based on experience and length of service and towards the incorporation of individual

performance into wage determination. In a 2002 survey by the MHWL, about 51 per cent of the companies surveyed had adopted elements of performance-based system and others were planning to do so.[5] The phasing in of these changes has not meant total abandonment of traditional principles and older workers are still paid more than younger ones. However, the bonus system is now being based more on individual contributions rather than on everyone of the same age or length of service receiving the same bonus.

Companies are also altering the way in which basic salaries are determined by including more performance-related elements, although a large number have experienced problems with this. In the MHWL survey, 88 per cent that had taken this course stated that they were experiencing implementation difficulties. The greatest problems cited were the difficulties involved in evaluating workers with different employment tasks (51.7 per cent), insufficient training of evaluators (49.4 per cent), unclear rating standards or the difficulty of setting these standards (42.8 per cent) and inability to determine performance differences because of over generous ratings (29.8 per cent).[6] Given that US companies experienced similar difficulties these problems are not surprising. In the United States it was often found that evaluating the highest and the lowest 10 per cent was possible, but attempting to evaluate meaningful differences in the middle 80 per cent was difficult.

Enterprise unions have played an active part in the changes described above, and this has had an effect on the distributive and procedural justice of the changes – in the case of distributive justice, giving ground on wage increase issues and retaining the elements of pay that are based on experience and length of service. With the unions input, those who are older or have had more experience with a firm generally earn more than those who are younger or less experienced. However, under the new system automatic annual pay increases according to age, experience and length of service can no longer be assumed in many companies. Nonetheless the fact that these changes in the wage system had to be worked out with the participation of enterprise unions points to importance of this pillar and its continued support of *Mikoshi* management.

Finally, we shall briefly discuss where changes are being applied in companies. For the most part it appears that for blue-collar workers companies are maintaining the traditional length of service/experience-based system. It is not at all clear why this should be the case since many blue-collar jobs are amenable to performance evaluation, whether on an assembly line or in a cell-based manufacturing system. It has been argued that because productivity can be measured more easily with blue-collar tasks, tracking of output is easier. In addition it has also been argued that blue-collar workers are motivated by peer or group pressure to perform better, which is consistent with the quality control and TQC (total quality control) approaches that have developed under the traditional system.

Also, companies wish their blue-collar workers to take on multiple tasks, such as quality control and the maintenance of machinery. Participation in total quality control and *kaizen* practices in most manufacturing companies is voluntary and the success of the measures is on the fact that the productivity improvements and sharing information inherent in them reassure workers that their jobs are secure, and this goes hand in hand with pay and promotion based on length of service. The savings made on wage costs by having these tasks carried out by trained workers far outweighs any benefits that might accrue from the implementation of performance-related pay.

Despite the above, some companies have introduced merit-based pay for blue-collar workers and moreover are employing temporary shop-floor workers from agencies such as Manpower (*Nikkei Sangyo Shimbun,* 14, July 2004) this formerly prohibited practice was facilitated by an amendment to the law on the dispatch of temporary workers in April 2004. Temporary production workers can now be brought in by manufacturing companies whenever they are needed. This, however, has disrupted the sense of community that existed under the *Mikoshi* system and it has proved difficult to set up voluntary teams that incorporate both temporary and regular workers (ibid.). With regard to white-collar jobs, this is the area in which Japanese management system has been seen as least effective in bringing about productivity improvements, so it is precisely at these jobs that individual merit systems are aimed.

Conclusions

What are the future prospects for *Mikoshi* management? Will it survive in its present form, converge with Western-style management or evolve into a new form of management system? Based on observations of changes that have taken place over the past ten years or so, some of which have been discussed above, we believe that during next five to ten years there will be further adjustments, but these will serve to maintain *Mikoshi* management. Even if some elements of the Japanese management system are fundamentally altered or abandoned, these second-order changes at one level will be undertaken to support stability of the core of *Mikoshi* management; that is, the company as an economic community of stakeholders. However, there will be difficulties that may introduce instabilities that in the long term may fundamentally alter the system.

The growth of temporary employment is already causing frictions where none existed previously. At the moment all temporary workers are Japanese, but in 20 years time the situation is likely to be different. Continuation of the birth rate (currently 1.28 for Japan as a whole and 0.98 in the Tokyo area) will reduce the number of Japanese graduates available for recruitment to large companies, the standard bearers of the Japanese management system. This will force companies to employ more women and bring more foreigners into management and especially into the upper management ranks. These changes may make simple adjustments at one level to support the continuity of the Mikoshi level less easy than before and may result in drastic alterations.

How the current generation of managers approach the following issues will likely be indicative of the path that *Mikoshi* management style takes in the future. The first is the increased participation of women. Presently women make up about 41 percent of the national workforce; they make up only about 9 percent of the managerial jobs, few of which are at the higher managerial level. How women are recruited, trained, socialized and promoted will affect the composition of those company employees who support the *Mikoshi* system and may well affect the concept of the company as an economic community of stakeholders. A recent study has indicated that companies that have taken a more supportive role in the promotion of woman into managerial ranks, have performed better in terms of sales and profits than companies that have been less open to women. The study goes on to indicate that it is not the women per se who are better managers, but that a culture within the company that supports women is more open to merit and performance issues and as a result both male and female managers who are more productive benefit. The implications for companies is evident in that it is the method by which managers are chosen for movement into and out of the *Mikoshi* that must be changed and not simply the promotion of women. This will inevitably lead to changes in the members of the *Mikoshi* and the importance of connections in the decision process of being promoted into the upper ranks of management.

A similar set of factors surrounds the second area of concern; the role that foreign companies and foreigner managers of Japanese companies will play. The apparent success of Carlos Ghosn and the placement of Sir Howard Stringer at the helm of Sony are perhaps indicative of the changes to come. How well the new chairman and chief executive of

Sony does in turning around the company will only be part of the story, as here too the way in which non-Japanese are recruited, socialized and promoted will play a large part in determining the fate of *Mikoshi* management.

The third issue is the role of younger and older Japanese managers as vectors of change. Venture companies and entrepreneurial start-ups are often seen as the realm of the young, but in Japan, entrepreneurs tend to be older, and are often retired managers (JSBRI, 2002). Entrepreneurial start-ups CRD, which is developing a new miniature disk drive, has been held up as an illustration of how to ensure the continued employment of workers who have reached retirement age in established companies (*Nikkei Sangyo Shinbum*, 6 July, 2004). Such companies will also have an impact on the employment choice of young people entering the workforce. Moreover, through greater competition for both younger and older workers, entrepreneurial companies may accelerate workforce adjustments at large companies. Although the latter will probably continue to be the most attractive proposition for both older and younger workers, employment in entrepreneurial start-ups will grow in appeal as the large companies continue to reduce their core work force of lifetime employees.

How this will affect *Mikoshi* management is difficult to predict. The adjustments made thus far in order to cope with change and uncertainty in the Japanese economy are helping to support the system. However, unintended consequences of these adjustments might overturn the system as a whole at some point in the future. One indication of this relates to leadership and the role of financial markets as a disciplinary constraint on managerial actions. The recent hostile takeover attempt by Livedoor of Nippon Broadcasting and Fuji Television, illustrates both an avenue for drastic change and also the reliance of the Japanese management system. There are several points of interest here. First it is an attempted hostile takeover of a reasonably healthy company, and as such is setting a precedent in its own right. Second, at first the approach taken by the initiator, Mr Horie, appeared to be rather brash and non-traditional, almost American in terms of takeover style. However, after he gained a controlling interest in Nippon Broadcasting he took a more conciliatory stance. Part of this change in tone may have arisen out of the reaction of Nippon Broadcastings employees who all signed documents supporting the current management and criticizing Livedoor's attempted takeover. In addition many of the customers and advertisers of Nippon Broadcasting, another stakeholder group, have criticized the attempt. The final result has been the reconciliation of the existing management, which still is in place, with Mr Horie as a member of the board of directors. The entire drama has also caused the government to re-examine the changes in the commercial code for gaining controlling interests in a company in order to prevent similar types of takeovers. This would potentially radically change the *Mikoshi* management. However, in order to gain real economic synergy out of the acquisition, Livedoor and Mr Horie must continue to work with the current set of stakeholders and as a result he has altered his tone and is perhaps realizing that owning is not the same as managing, at least not in the current configuration of Japanese management style.[7]

It is most likely that the changes we have discussed will alter the composition of management. There will probably be more women and foreigners, and there will be greater scope for younger managers to advance, but the core of the *Mikoshi* system the firm as an economic community rather than a vehicle to maximize shareholder wealth, is not likely to change drastically in the foreseeable future.

The way in which the new Japanese management system is emerging is very Japanese in style in that it involves building a consensus around what will best benefit the group. Lifetime employment is still seen as having economic as well as social merit and attempts will be made to maintain it. How the employment security associated with it will be provided by one company for life or by several companies, and who that security will be provided for is unclear. What happens to the governance and leadership systems in Japanese companies will also be important to watch. The move towards greater transparency will continue and equity markets will play a larger part in constraining management power. But whether this will make companies a vehicle for shareholder wealth maximization as opposed to economic communities of employees is open to question. Will these be a re-emergence of 'Taisho democracy', not only in the political sense but also in its more market-based aspects, but without the excesses that led to its being rejected by Japan as too chaotic?

Notes

1. See Nikkei Business Express, www.nb.nikkei.bp.co,jp/members/project/20040617/106104.
2. The recent attempt by Livedoor to take over Nippon Broadcasting in order to gain access to Fuji Television is an example of a hostile attempt to take over a 'healthy' company. One reason the activities of the main agents have generated so much media attention is the fact that these types of hostile take over activity have been rare. We shall discuss the implications of this later in the chapter.

3. It should be noted that Daiei's bankruptcy has more to do with its overexpansion during the bubble period than to integrating part-time work into its human resource management system.
4. For general employment practices see www.itoyokado.iyg.co.jp/company/ eco/pdfs/ItoYokadoCSR2003_p32-33.pdf; for employment practices related to women see www.itoyokado.iyg.co.jp/company/eco/pdfs/ItoYokado CSR2003_p34.pdf.
5. Survey of Employment Management, www.dbtk.mhlw.go.jp/toukei/kouhyo/ indexkr_2_1.html, Table 14.
6. Survey of Employment Management, www.dbtk.mhlw.go.jp/toukei/kouhyo/ indexkr_2_3.html, Table 26.
7. Son of Softbank is acting as the white knight in this drama, but he is not an insider. He belongs neither to the Fujisankei group, to which Fuji Television and Nippon Broadcasting belong, nor to the corporate world. His role must be played out with the other stakeholders in mind.

References

Appold, S.J., S Siengthai, J.D. Kasarda (1998) 'The Employment of Women Managers and Professional in an Emerging Economy: Gender Inequality as an Organizational Practice', *Administrative Science Quarterly*, 43 (3), pp. 538–65.
Aoki, M. (1990) 'Towards an Economic Model of the Japanese Firm', *Journal of Economic Literature*, 38 (1), pp. 1–27.
Argyris, C. (1976) 'Single- and double-loop models in research on decision-making', *Administrative Science Quarterly* 21 (3), pp. 363–375.
Argyris, C. (1992) *On Organizational Learning*, Cambridge, MA: Blackwell Publishing, Inc.
Ashby, W.R. (1952) *Design for a Brain*, New York: Wiley.
Cole, R.E. (1972) 'Permanent Employment in Japan: Fact and Fantasies', *Industrial and Labor Relations Review*, 26 (1), pp. 615–630.
Cole, R.E. (1972). 'Functional Alternatives and Economic Development: An Empirical Example of Permanent Employment in Japan', *American Sociological Review*, 38 (4), pp. 424–438.
Dunphy, D. (1987) 'Convergence/Divergence: a temporal review of the Japanese enterprise and its management', *The Academy of Management Review*, 12 (3), pp. 445–459.
Edwards, L. N. (1988) 'Equal Employment Opportunity in Japan: A View from the West', *Industrial and Labor Relations Review*, 41 (2), pp. 240–250.
Gersick, C.J. (1991) 'Revolutionary Change Theories: A Multilevel Exploration of the Punctuated Equilibrium Paradigm', *Academy of Management Review*, 16 (1), pp. 10–36.
Hanai, K. (July 26, 2004 'Lifting women's job status' *The Japan Times*, p.16', for general employment practices see http://www.itoyokado.iyg.co.jp/ company/eco/pdfs/ItoYokadoCSR2003_p32-33.pdf; for employment practices related to women see http://www.itoyokado.iyg.co.jp/company/eco/pdfs/ ItoYokadoCSR2Q03_ p34.pdf.
Hirakubo, N. (1999) 'The End of Lifetime Employment in Japan', *Business Horizon*, 42 (6), pp. 41–46.
Inohara, Hideo (1990) *Human Resource Development in Japanese Companies*, Asian Productivity Organization, Tokyo.

Jones, H.J. (1976) 'Japanese Women and the Dual-Track Employment System', *Pacific Affairs*, 49 (4), pp. 589–606.

JSBRI (2002) *White Paper on Small and Medium Enterprises in Japan: The age of the local entrepreneur-birth, growth and revitalization of the national economy*. Japan Small Business Research Institute, METI Tokyo Japan.

Katz, Richard (1998) *Japan the System that Soured: The Rise and Fall of the Japanese Economic Miracle*, M.E. Sharpe, NY.

Lincoln, Edward J. (2001) *Arthritic Japan: The Slow Pace of Economic Reform*, Brookings Institution Press, Washington, D.C.

Methé, D.T. (2005) "Continuity through Change in Japanese Management: Institutional and Strategic Influences in R.Haak (ed) *Japanese Management – The Search for a New Balance between Continuity and Change*". Palgrave, London UK.

Morel B. and R. Ramanujam, (1999) 'Through the Looking Glass of Complexity: The Dynamics of Organizations as Adapting and Evolving Systems', *Organization Science* 10 (3), pp. 278–293.

Ministry of Health, Welfare and Labour (1987, 1992, 1997, 2002) *Employment Status Surveys Ministry of Health*, Welfare and Labour, Ministry of Health, Labour and Welfare, Tokyo, Japan.

Ministry of Health, Labour and Welfare (2003) *White Paper on the Labour Economy 2003: Economic and Social Change and Diversification of Working Styles*, Ministry of Health, Labour and Welfare, Tokyo, Japan.

METI (2003) *Challenges and Directions of Economic and Industrial Policy in Japan*, November 2003 METI, Tokyo, Japan.

Nikkei Business Express June 17, 2004 http://nb.nikkeibp.co.jp/members/Proiect/20040617/106104.

Nihon Keizai Shinbun, June 28, 2004 'Kikan toshikaGian ni hantai, kiken fueru', p.15.

Nihon Keizai Shimbun, 'Ni Chu Kan FTA Hitsuyo 7 Wari: Sankakoku keieisha san byaku nin chosa', March, 24, 2004 pp.1 (Japan-China-Korea FTA 70 percent necessary: survey of 300 CEOs in those three countries)

Nikkei Ryutsu Shimbun April 25, 2002 p.11 'Otei supa pato karishoku ni sekkyoku toyo Daiei, Yokado'.

Nihon Keizai Shimbun, June 18, 2004 "Shorai freeter ni naru kamo shin nyu sha in no 3 wari" p.42.

Nikkei Sangyo Shimbun November 8, 2002 'Toshiba ga shanai FA sei Shanai koubo mo kakudai' (Toshiba introduces employee FA System and extends internal disclosure of vacant positions and internal recruitment).

Nikkei Sangyo Shimbun, July 6, 2004 'CRD utilizing the expertise of retired skilled workers as a solution to the aging society' p. 22.

Nikkei Sangyo Shimbun April 10, 2001 'Fujitsu sekashingin no hyoka minaoshi gyomu process mo koryo' p. 27 and May 18, 2001 'Daini stage mukaeta sekashugi Fujitsu hyoka hohou o bapon kaikaku hikui mokuhyo urusanai' p. 25.

Nikkei Sangyo Shimbun, July 14, 2004 "QC sa-kuru no siren"p.24.

Nonaka, I. (1988) 'Towards Middle-Up-Down Management: Accelerating Information Creation', *Sloan Management Review*, pp. 9–18.

Royalty, A. B. (1996). 'The Effects of Job Turnover on the Training of Men and Women', *Industrial and Labor Relations Review*, 49 (3), pp. 506–21.

Sakano, T., A.Y. Lewin (1999). 'Impact of CEO Succession in Japanese Companies: A Coevolutionary Perspective', *Organizational Science*, 10 (5), pp. 654–71.

Schein, V.E., R. Mueller, T. Lituchy and J. Liu (1996) 'Think Manager–Think Male: A Global Phenomenon?', *Journal of Organizational Behavior*, 17 (1), pp. 33–41.

Sugimoto, Y. (2003) *An Introduction to Japanese Society*, 2nd edn, Cambridge: Cambridge University Press.

Survey of Employment Management, MHWL, Times Series Table 14, http://wwwdbtk.mhlw.go.jp/toukei/kouhyo/indexkr_2_l.html.

Survey of Employment Management, Table 26 2002 Survey MHWL, http://http://wwwdbtk.mhlw.go.jp/toukei/kouhvo/indexkr_2_3.html.

9
Managing the Development of One's Own Vocational Skills

Hiroyuki Fujimura

Introduction

This chapter explains why the development of one's own vocational skills has become so important in Japan, and outlines the way in which individuals try to enhance those skills.

During the period of high economic growth from the end of World War II to the early 1990s Japanese society placed great value on stable employment. However the collapse of the bubble economy and the prolonged recession that followed forced Japanese companies to relinquish their cherished policy of employment security and make significant cuts in their workforce. The growing awareness of individuals that they must develop their vocational skills is related to this development.[1]

The share of regular employees in firms' total workforce is dropping every year. According to Labour Force Surveys, on average the share declined from 76.8 per cent in February 1997 to 69.5 per cent in December 2002. Regular employees are defined as those with an indefinite employment contract. Under Japan's labour laws they are in little danger of being laid off, so in that sense their employment is stable. On the other hand employees with fixed-term contracts may not have their contracts renewed upon expiry, so their employment is unstable. Indeed survey results show that about 10 per cent of those who leave their jobs do so because their contract has expired.

Employees with relatively stable employment could once assume that their vocational training would take place principally within the company at which they worked. In most companies employees were regularly transferred to new posts and learnt particular skills at each one. Employees of large companies were often seconded or transferred to subsidiaries or affiliated companies before they reached the retirement age of 60. In all cases employment security was practically guaranteed.

However the economic recession has considerably weakened the employment security safeguards once offered by companies. The collapse of Hokkaido Takushoku Bank, the voluntary liquidation of Yamaichi Securities and the effective dismantling of Snow Brand after a food poisoning scandal and subsidy fraud have fuelled people's anxiety as no one knows which will be the next large firm to fall bankrupt. Thus employees now have to contemplate the possibility of having to look for another job, and consequently they have to pay attention to the skills they have to offer prospective employers.

Training and employability

Combining on-the-job and off-the-job training

In general, training in Japan begins at home with the learning of common social rules that must be obeyed. At school pupils learn not only academic subjects but also acquire the ability to think, communicate and behave as a member of a group. Once employed, individuals learn through on-the-job training (OJT) and by dealing with daily events and problems (see Koike, 1999, for details). There is doubt about the value of OJT in the development skills, but to review acquired skills or to compete in a new line of work, off-the-job training is required. The duration of this depends on the objective. If the objective is to review existing skills a period of a few days to a week is more than adequate. However if it is to obtain new knowledge or skills a longer period, perhaps including postgraduate study, is required. The question is whether it is possible to combine on-the-job and off-the-job training effectively.[2]

When considering OJT there are three points to keep in mind: whether it involves the same company or a number of companies, whether the training is organized (follows a plan, involves superior, and so on), and personal motivation (whether the individual takes the initiative to develop his or her career) Points to be borne in mind in the case of off-the-job training are location, content, goals and duration.

Employability

Now that long-term employment in one company can no longer be guaranteed, individuals have to pay attention to their employability – that is, the possession of skills that can be transferred from one company to another. Those who believe that employability depends on the techniques and skills that a person possesses stress the importance of gaining public certification and undergoing vocational training, while the Japanese Trade Union Confederation (1999, pp. 7–8) proposes that employability refers both to 'skills that enable worker mobility' and to 'skills that are demonstrated in a company and that enable a worker to be employed on a continous basis'. Both definitions stress that enhancing skills improves employability.

Matsumote *et al.* (2001) have constructed an employability checklist with eight criteria, under which there are nine or ten categories for self-evaluation. The criteria are (1) communication skills, (2) interpersonal skills, (3) organizing and running an organization, (4) cognitive ability/concept-making ability, (5) learning ability, (6) mental toughness, (7) response to changes and (8) self-sufficiency and self-enhancement. An employability rating is established by deciding where one fits on a scale of one to five. While assessing one's employability is very important, there still are a number of factors that need to be considered, such as the reciprocity among the various criteria and the validity of the categories within each criterion.

This chapter analyzes employability in terms of the skills people need to change jobs halfway through their career. If we examine the questions that are asked during interviews, the criteria of employability should become obvious and therefore it should be possible to devise a combination of on-the-job and off-the-job training for skill enhancement.

How companies and employees view skill development

This section draws on two surveys: a vocational ability development survey commissioned by the Ministry of Health, Labour and Welfare and carried out by the Japan Institute of Labour in November and December 2001; and a survey on long-term leave for vocational development. The latter (hereafter referred to as the Fuji survey) was carried out by the Fuji Researches Institute in March 2000 on behalf of the Ministry of Health, Labour and Welfare. Both surveys had separate questionnaires for companies and employees. The former garnered responses from 2176 companies and 5658 employees, and the latter received responses from 1099 companies and 3103 employees. Since the companies in the surveys differed in size, the result differed slightly as well. Of the companies that responded to the vocational ability development survey, 89.6 per cent were small and medium-sized with fewer than 300 employees, while those the Fuji surveyed were principally large and 29.7 per cent had more than 1000 employees. It would be appropriate, then, to draw on vocational ability development survey to capture the situation in small companies and on the Fuji survey to obtain an idea of conditions in large companies.

Views on who should be responsible for vocational training

Almost 70 per cent of the companies that responded to the Fuji survey stated that the company had traditionally been responsible for vocational training, but nearly half thought that in the future this should be the responsibility of employees (Figure 9.1). The larger the company the more obvious this tendency became. For companies with more than 2000 regular employees (133 of the respondents), 78.2 per cent stated that the company had been responsible but only 30.8 per cent said they would continue to be so. For companies with fewer than 300 employees (242 of the respondents) these proportions were 65.3 per cent and 56.2 per cent respectively, a very small difference. The same trend was evident in the vocational ability development survey. With regard to what employees thought, can be seen in Figure 9.1 a high proportion believed that vocational training should be their responsibility and around two thirds were already taking steps to develop their skills. There was little difference among age groups in this respect.

While it is important for employees to have a positive attitude towards personal responsibility for vocational training, whether they are taking appropriate action is another matter. We shall return to this issue later.

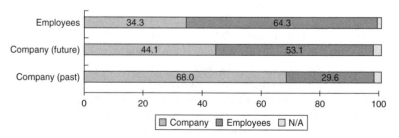

Source: Fuji Research Institute (2000).

Figure 9.1 Survey results of who has been/should be responsible for vocational training (per cent)

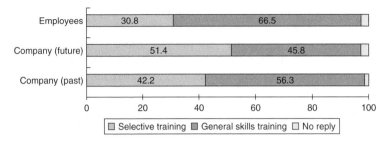

Source: Fuji Research Institute (2000).

Figure 9.2   Opinions on employee training policies

Selective *versus* general training

Figure 9.2 shows the survey results on whether training should be
targeted at a select band of employees or all employees. As can be seen,
on this point, there was a significant difference between the opinions of
employees and companies. Over 50 per cent of the companies were
planning to move towards selective training,[3] but nearly 67 per cent of
employees wished to continue to receive general skills training. Thus it
appears that while employees believed they should become responsible
for the development of certain skills they still expected their companies
to provide them with basic training.

Effective ways of conducting OJT

It was noted earlier that there are three points to bear in mind when
considering OJT: whether the same company or a number of companies
are involved, the way in which training is organized, and personal
motivation to develop one's own career. A number of surveys have been
conducted on the practical aspects of OJT but they are not sufficiently
wide-ranging to be of value here. Therefore we shall continue to draw on
the two surveys used above, plus one conducted by the Japanese Trade
Union confederation in 1999 (hereafter referred to as the JTUC survey).[4]

Experience gained at other companies and during interdepartmental transfers

The respondents in the JTUC survey were asked whether experience
gained at another company was useful in their present job. Of the 3194
respondents who had worked at other companies, 13.5 per cent considered that their previous experience was very useful in their present job,
36.0 per cent thought that it was useful to some extent and 23.7 per cent

said it was not useful. Of the 4230 employees who had had interdepartmental transfers at their current company, 14.1 per cent said the experienced gained was very useful, 52.4 per cent thought it was useful to some extent and 19.0 per cent stated that it was not useful. It is notable that experience gained at other companies was rated almost as highly as experience gained from interdepartmental transfers. However these figures reflect only the general impressions of the respondents and individual case studies are required to determine the nature of the usefulness of each kind of experience.

Guidance and skill cultivation by superiors

The Fuji survey provides indirect information on organized training as part of OJT. Companies were asked the following question: 'Do you think that immediate superiors fulfil the role of advisor when an employee is considering career development?' Four replies were provided, ranging from 'Yes' (6.8 per cent of companies) to 'No'; 37.8 per cent replied that 'It is more accurate to say the immediate superior is fulfilling such a role than to say that he/she is not', raising the total percentage of companies where superiors were fulfilling a career advisory role to 44.6 per cent. This percentage increased with company size. For example 51.1 per cent of companies with 2000 or more employees stated that this was the case, but only 41.8 per cent of companies with fewer than 300 employees did so. The fact that less than half of all superiors were considered to be fulfilling advisory roles raises concern that OJT may not be functioning well.

The Fuji survey did not explore the kind of guidance superiors gave, but the individual section of the vocational ability development survey investigated both this and the usefulness of the advice. As shown in Figure 9.3, the most common guidance was on responsibility for a specific task (44.1 per cent) followed by getting the employee to consider a plan to improve operations (36.0 per cent). By age group, the most common advice provided to employees 24 years old and younger was about work and about their life or attitude to work (both 38.3 per cent), while for people in their late thirties or older it was getting them to consider a plan to improve operations.

It was judged that the most useful guidance was on responsibility for a specific task (20.0 per cent), advice about work (16.7 per cent) and getting the employee to attempt more difficult/complicated work (14.5 per cent). Only 8.5 per cent of supervisors attempted to get the employee to consider a plan to improve operations. Considering ways to improve operations can be an effective way of enhancing vocational skills, but if

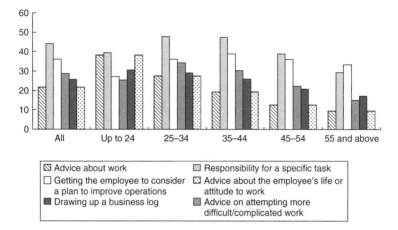

Note: Multiple answers were allowed.

Source: Vocational ability development survey.

Figure 9.3 Guidance provided to employees by superiors, by age group (per cent)

superiors do not properly explain the goals and benefits of this, employees may feel that their already heavy work load is being increased and that they are too busy to put much effort into it. It is therefore necessary for superiors to put more thought into the matter.

The motivation of employees

The Fuji survey asked firms what percentage of their employees were considering taking the initiative for their own career development (Figure 9.4). It also asked employees about the extent to which they had a concrete vision of the future (Figure 9.5). Just 8.1 per cent of companies thought that almost all or 80 per cent of their employees intended to take this initiative. The majority (63.5 per cent) replied that only 25–50 per cent of their employees were taking steps to develop their careers. Thus in general companies did not think that employees were likely to be aggressive about developing their careers. As for the employees themselves, just 8.7 per cent had concrete plans for the future ('In *x* years I will be doing this'). While 49.2 per cent claimed to be vaguely thinking about their future, this was essentially the same as not considering it at all. Hence less than 10 per cent had concrete thoughts about their future working lives, and it is likely that independent skill development will end up being nothing more than a slogan.

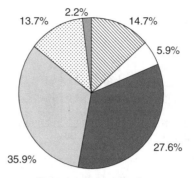

Percentage of companies

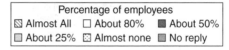

Source: Fuji Research Institute (2000).

Figure 9.4 Employers' estimates of the percentage of employees who were taking the initiative for their own career development

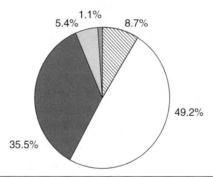

Source: Fuji Research Institute (2000).

Figure 9.5 Extent to which employees were considering their future working lives

Effective ways of conducting off the-job training

As stated earlier, there are four important aspects to off-the-job training: location, content, awareness of goals and duration. As these are closely interrelated, ideally the discussion should incorporate data that provide an overview of them in combination. However no such data are available so we shall have to examine them separately.

Merits and demerits of in-house training and training by external organizations

Figure 9.6 shows companies' and employees' responses to the question of where training should take place. As can be seen, 60 per cent of the companies preferred in-house training but were planning to use external education and training organizations to a greater extent in the future. On the other hand the majority of employees (60 per cent) placed greater importance on external training. It seems that this was because they believed that training received within the company would not be useful if they moved to another company, whereas training received from an external institution would be generally applicable. There is no way of confirming this supposition, but there can be no doubt that job insecurity affected employees' responses.

The JTUC survey examined the perceived usefulness of in-house and external training. According to 37.5 per cent of the employees surveyed the most useful training was that received from an external; 23.3 per cent thought that in-house training was more effective; and 7.2 per cent considered that formal classes within the company best suited their needs. Looking at the results by company size, the percentage of employees who responded that being sent outside the company for training was more

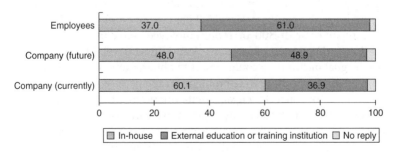

Source: Fuji Research Institute (2000).

Figure 9.6 Preferred location of off-the-job training (per cent)

useful was higher for small companies than for large ones. This is probably because large companies have better education and training facilities. However, whether such training is always useful depends on the content of the training and the skill level of the trainee being well matched.

Content of education and training

The effectiveness of training depends on the individual employee, so it is not possible to determine whether each detail of a training pro-gramme is useful and we shall therefore have to generalize. The JTUC survey asked employees to specify what kind of training had been of help to them. The most common reply was training to master basic skills related to work (30.6 per cent), followed by training to deepen specialist knowledge related to work (23.8 per cent), training to master a general skill, such as leadership (18.1 per cent) and training to obtain a certificate related to work (9.8 per cent). What is notable is that the enhancement of basic skills was appreciated more than mastering specific skills.

Goal awareness

While there is no information on the goals of employees who partici-pate in off-the-job training the vocational ability development survey did examine why employees seek self-enhancement. Self-enhancement is one form of off-the-job training and many companies provide support for it in the form of subsidies or by adjusting working hours to enable class attendance: 81.1 per cent of the companies that took part in the survey provided some kind of support.[5]

The most common reasons why employees tried to better themselves were to obtain the knowledge and skills necessary for their current job (79.5 per cent), to prepare for future work and career advancement (38.8 per cent) and to obtain a certificate (34.1 per cent). Considering the responses by company size, 51.2 per cent of employees who worked for companies with 300 or more employees took part in off-the-job training in the interest of future work and career development. This very specific goal meant they could expect to obtain more benefits from their training. However there were problems in the path of many employees. Some were too busy to engage: self-enhancement (43.0 per cent), a number thought that too many expenses were incurred (25.9 per cent), a number of companies did not allow employees to take leave or go home early (18.3 per cent), it was difficult to obtain information on seminars and the like (15.3 per cent) and the results of self-enhancement courses were not valued enough by the company (15.2 per cent).

Duration of training

Off-the-job training is more effective if it takes place over a fairly long period of time, particularly in the case of learning new skills that are difficult to acquire at the place of work. The Fuji survey investigated companies' and employees' attitudes towards taking leave for vocational training. When asked about their response to employees' requests to take leave to develop their skills, more than half the companies replied that they did nothing and about a third said that they instructed the employees to use their holiday time. Only 3.1 per cent provided special leave for vocational training, and 6 per cent of treated such leave as unpaid. Hence the majority were negative about leave for vocational training.

Recently the number of companies that allow leave for voluntary activities has increased. The time taken off work for this is in addition to the regular annual leave. Generally the leave only amounts to a few days a year, but if the employee is participating in the Japan Overseas Cooperation Volunteers a maximum of two and a half years is allowed. There are two reasons why companies allow this kind of long-term leave: it appeals to the companies' sense of social responsibility, and they feel that catering to the diverse needs of employees helps to attract outstanding employees. Unpaid leave for vocational training and long-term leave for voluntary work probably cannot be lumped together, but if they are viewed in terms of responding to the diverse needs of employees there is not that much difference between them. The Fuji survey revealed that about 40 per cent of employees would like to take long-term leave to study, and it appears that some companies were planning some kind of support for employees' long-term learning activities.[6]

The analysis in this section of on-the-job and off-the-job training suggests the following conclusions:

- Both companies and employees are starting to believe that employees should be responsible for developing their own skills.
- Companies tend to place importance on selective training, while employees prefer general skills training.
- Many employees think that acquiring experience at other companies is useful for their present job.
- Many superiors do not consider it their duty to give career advice.
- Only a small number of employees have concrete plans for their career development, which goes against the belief that employees should be responsible for their own vocational training.

- There is a strong tendency among employees to prefer to receive education and training outside the company.
- It is thought that training to master basic vocational skills is more useful than learning specialized skills.
- While many employees do wish to take steps to improve themselves in order to attain concrete goals, time and cost restrictions are preventing them from doing so.
- Employees look favourably on long-term leave to develop their skills, but companies tend to be negative about this.

Cultivating transferable skills

One way to identity which skills are needed by employees who have to change companies is to study what companies focus on during job application interviews. When interviewing people applying for a mid-career position, interviewers ask questions such as the following:

- What types of company have you worked for previously?
- What work were you in charge of at each company?
- What was your role in projects that you have participated in recently?
- In what ways were those projects successful or unsuccessful?
- How did you benefit from taking charge of those projects?

Most interviews focus on the applicant's work experience. Questions on projects in which the applicant has been involved are emphasized because it is the only way an interviewer can obtain a clear idea of the applicant's skills.

The department to which a mid-career applicant might be assigned is usually taken into account during the screening and skills assessment process. An interviewer who works in the same field as the applicant can usually judge the skills and ability of the applicant even if they are meeting for the first time. It is important to be able to discuss one's previous work experience objectively during the mid-career employment interview.

For those who are likely to have to change jobs in mid-career it is important that they take stock of their skills and enhance those which can be utilized by other companies. Some aspects of work are often specific to individual companies. For example *nemawashi* process (the internal negotiations that take place before company decisions are made) tends to be company specific and the associated skills are not directly transferable. However practices that appear to differ from company to company may have some common threads and therefore skills can be adapted to a different working environment. To this end employees should try to obtain an overview of the entire work process in their present company. If they understand the part they play in the functioning of the organization they will be more able to develop appropriate methods of working efficiently and thereby improve the transferability of their skills.

Conclusions

Japanese companies were traditionally responsible for cultivating their employees' skills and careers. Skills were developed through day-to-day tasks and it was the company that decided what kind of work employees were assigned to and when. The later generally accepted transfers because they understood that this would contribute to the development of their skills and benefit their career. The frequent personnel transfers were conducted on the basis of a relationship of trust between companies and employees.

However this relationship of trust is on the point of collapse. It is naturally unacceptable for employees who have been obediently adhering to their company's requests for more than 20 years to be told, that their skills are no longer useful to the company and therefore they should leave. It might be more acceptable if re-employment were arranged, but this rarely happens. Young employees are well aware of the outrageous treatment of middle-aged and elderly employees, and knowing that they may be treated the same way in the future is resulting in a decline in their work and commitment.

Now that companies are no longer taking responsibility for employees until retirement age, many are highlighting the importance of self-responsibility in skills cultivation. Thus employees have become responsible for managing their daily work and finding new challenges. To do this, information and good judgment are necessary. If daily on-the-job training were made more systematic and off-the-job training were incorporated into the programme – enabling employees to improve their information-gathering skills and their ability to analyze information – employees would be able to develop skills that were not only useful to the present employer but could also be utilized by other companies in the event of redundancy. According to the Japanese Federation of Employers two types of skill are essential to employability: skills that enable worker mobility and skills that are specific to a certain company and enable the worker to be employed on a continuous basis. These skills are in fact not separate but overlap, and in combination they can aid employment security.

Notes

1. In a survey conducted by The Works Institute, Recruitment Company (2003), 56.5 per cent of the respondents claimed to be worried about keeping their jobs. The figures for regular employees were 55.4 per cent for males and 46.8 per cent for females.
2. The effectiveness of incorporating short-term off-the-job training into OJT is described in Koike (1999), pp. 43–6.
3. There were large differences according to company size. In the case of companies with 2000 or more employees, only 18.8 per cent had previously concentrated on selective training but 78.2 per cent intended to do so in future. In contrast 36.8 per cent of companies with fewer than 300 employees had provided selective training and 39.7 per cent planned to do so in future. The vocational ability development survey asked the same question but the percentage of companies planning to concentrate on selective training (34.1 per cent) was smaller than the percentage that had done so in the past (40.1 per cent). This shows that small companies intend to continue to place importance on general skills training.
4. This survey was conducted through the industrial trade unions affiliated to the confederation. There were 6573 respondents.
5. Subsidies are provided by individual companies, the national education and training benefit system, and unions. The national education and training benefit system was established in 1998 and is used by many people. Among the respondents to the vocational ability development survey, 5.6 per cent replied that they had benefited from this system. However its full usefulness has not yet been properly evaluated.
6. In Europe there are schemes that allow employees to take long-term leave to develop their vocational skills (Arbeit und Leben, 1999). For example in Denmark employees can take a year's paid leave for education and training.

References

Arbeit und Leben (1999) *Paid Educational Leave in Europe. A Strategy Promoting Lifelong Learning?* (Düsseldorf).

Fuji Research Institute (2000) *Noryoku Kaihatsu to no Katsudo ni Torikumu tame no Choki Kyuka Seido no Donyu Sokushin ni Muketa Chosa Kenkyu* (Research Survey Aimed at Promoting the Introduction of a Long-Term Leave System for Developing Vocational Skills and Other Activities) (Fuji Research Institute).

Fujimura, H. (2000) 'Shakaiteki ni Tsuyo Suru Noryoku wo Takameru Hoho' (Ways to Increase Skills that Can be Utilized in Society), *Kinro Yokohama*, July–August, pp. 3–11.

Koike, K. (1999) *Shigoto no Keizaigaku* (The Economics of Work), 2nd edn (Tokyo: Toyo Keizai Shinposha).

Japan Institute of Labour (2000) *Noryoku Kaihatsu Kihon Chosa Hokokusho* (Development of Vocational Skills, Basic Survey Report) (Tokyo: Japan Institute of Labour).

Japanese Trade Union Confederation (1999) *Enpuroiabiriti no Kakuritsu wo mezashite: 'Jugyoin Jiritsu, Kigyo Shien-gata' no Jinzai Ikusei wo* (Aiming to Establish Employability: Cultivating Human Resources through Self-sufficiency of Employees and Company Support) (Tokyo: Japanese Trade Union Confederation).

Matsumoto, S., C. Asai, H. Tajima and T. Kinoshita (2001) 'Tajigen Kigyo Miryoku Shakudo to Enpuroiabiriti Chekkurisuto no Shisaku Kenkyu' (Research into the Degree of Attractiveness of Multidimensional Companies and Employability Checklists), *Kenkyu Kiyo*, 21, pp. 1–41.

Research Institute for the Advancement of Living Standards (2000) *Kinrosha no Kyaria Keisei no Jittai to Ishiki ni kan suru Chosa Hokokusho* (Survey Report on the Present State and Awareness of Career Development of Workers) (Tokyo: Research Institute for the Advancement of Living Standards).

Works Institute Recruitment Company (2003) *Waakingu Paason Chosa 2002 [Shutoken]* (Working Person Survey 2002, Tokyo Metropolitan Area) (Tokyo: Works Institute Recruitment Co.).

10
The Shift Towards a Performance-Based Management System: From *Noryokushugi* to *Seikashugi*

Philippe Debroux

Introduction: origin and development of the Japanese wage system

In the period immediately after World War II, family composition and tenure were key elements with wage curves based on the concept of living wage taking into account employees' needs during the different stages of their life (Magota, 1970). Companies were unhappy from the start with this model, which they felt provided too few incentives for efficiency, leading to a distorted internal allocation of pay funds. The large majority of workers could be sure that they would keep their job regardless of their performance and moreover could expect an automatic yearly pay increase. This meant that the payroll total rose automatically even without the addition of new workers (Koshiro, 2000).

Although the system changed slightly over time, it was only in the 1970s that the weighting of the living-cost and seniority elements was significantly reduced and that of work-related factors increased. This followed the adoption of the *shokuno shikaku seido*, the grading system that had been advocated by Nikkeiren management since the mid 1960s. According to Nikkeiren (1969) the Japanese economy needed an HRM system that encouraged the optimization of employees skills by rewarding skills and performance and not derived from academic credentials, age or tenure. In that sense, the introduction of the skill-grading system was perceived by management as marking the belated end of the 'war period'. Using the term *noryokushugi*, that can be loosely translated as a system 'based on a test of capabilities' and accumulated experience and training, Nikkeiren's proposal was a clever response to overcome the rigidities of the HRM system, while reflecting the Japanese socioeconomic and cultural environment of the time in terms of fairness, equity and motivation. Abilities and skills cultivated over the long term perspective were to become the most important elements of the wage structure. Its objective was to eliminate or minimize the bias towards seniority and encourage competition in the internal labour market, while keeping a welfare corporatist system under which the large corporations undertook some of the functions that would be fulfilled by government in Europe and even in the United States.

Indeed, the Japanese social security system improved considerably, but, despite its growing affluence Japan did not become a welfare state after World War II. By the end of the 1960s, welfare corporatism had become so strongly legitimized socially and economically that it could not be challenged easily. Accordingly the wish of companies to develop an HRM system based on contingent labour-management relationships regulated on a free grading external labour market could not be realized. Despite the high level of operational ability the system created, it could be argued that it was its connotation with welfare corporatism that explains why it was increasingly difficult to apply efficiently when economic growth started to slow down and the ageing process accelerated. It was prone from the start to drift back to a seniority-based system. The slowing down of the economy in the 1970s reinforced managements' perception that consolidating the welfare corporatist agreement with the in-house unions was more than ever a key factor in business success. As a result remuneration was never considered as a straight compensation for labour. The link with the living wage concept was never cut. Consideration of age, family composition and tenure were not completely removed from the basic wage, and allowances linked to family, housing, transportation and so on continued to be paid. Under the grading system, the ability-based part of the wage was increased but in most companies it never amounted to more than about 50 per cent of the total for both blue- and white-collar workers. In order to keep the income differential low, in most large companies overlapping was maintained on the wage levels of employees with different ranking. Wage groups did not stack neatly one on top of another in a salary structure, showing that seniority remained built into the system, in contradiction of the objective of creating distinctions according to ability and skill. An across-the-board increase of the skill and ability-based part of the wage became a standard item in the yearly negotiations with the unions. It was considered as a given that a rise in marginal labour productivity was the result of a continuous process of specific training and new skill development gained through job rotation and on-the-job training. Therefore, the rationale was that a series of upward steps in wage-tenure profile was the natural return of the gains in human capital productivity. The (unrealistic) assumptions were that the ability of all workers rose at the same rate every year and that no skills became obsolescent. Coupled with the necessity of maintaining long-term economic incentives through promotion in the internal labour market, this led to the creation of ranks and subranks, which were meaningless in terms of measuring skill acquisition and assigning jobs but raised labour costs.

The shift towards *Seikashugi*

The skill-grading salary system is still dominant in large companies, but they accelerate the pace of change when raising the actual performance-based content of wages (Sueki, 2003). A growing number of companies are shifting partly or completely away from their traditional grading system because they believe it is based on an obsolete ideology of working relationships, and therefore it is not only a question of improving its implementation. In fact in many companies there has long been a gradual decline in the importance placed on age and tenure and greater emphasis on individual performance and job-related factors in wage setting. These changes could (and still are) made within the framework of the skill-grading system and it is likely that it will remain the case for some categories of workers.

The current HRM reforms should be viewed as part of the changes in the Japanese business system and society at large. At both the macro- and the microeconomic level, political and business leaders emphasize the necessity of gradually transforming what is perceived as the unqualified worker's 'rights' to social and economic benefits into a more conditional 'contract' between donors and recipients based on one form or other of mutual obligation and, in the end, only to a contingent right. The most significant regulatory initiatives on the part of public authorities have been to facilitate the creation of a more market-centred business system. Competition policy and regulatory reforms are expected to create new market opportunities in releasing competition. These opportunities will be exploited only if company reform mends the rents perceived to have developed in the business system. Although it may not completely converge with Anglo-Saxon corporate governance principles, the intention is to make HRM more attuned to the growing importance companies must accord to shareholder value and to the sociocultural changes in work and career expectations.

Changes are expected to be gradual because compromises must be made in order to keep the whole system stable. However even in this case the adoption of management concepts derived from what is called *seikashugi* which can be translated as 'actual performance-based evaluation and reward system', is claimed by companies to be a departure from the welfare corporatist ideology. Companies that insist on the moral obligation of a job guaranteed until retirement for their regular employees regardless of the shift towards more market-centred corporate governance may become a minority (Kokura, 1999). This is not to say that there is no pressure on them to honour their social obligations to their employees. Although casually practiced by SME, laying-off of regular employees for mere economic convenience is still frowned upon by the business establishment, and this can be expected to remain the case for large companies (Okuda, 2001). But the trend towards a smaller core of regular employees and greater and more diversified use of non-regular workers and outsourcing is bound to grow. Most of those who have adopted *seikashugi*-type reforms coupled with a long-term human capital development put emphasis on the economic advantages of a long-term HRM perspective as exemplified by a recent declaration by Nippon Keidanren (2004). The business establishment still considers that the key to create and sustain competitive advantages is more than ever a skilled and long-term committed workforce. As declared, long-term human capital development strategy is not incompatible, quite the contrary, with drastic changes in HRM, including greater use of performance-related pay and a wider use of the external labour market (*Financial Times*, 18 December 2003). Companies expect (and even encourage) a higher turnover in their workforce, including managers. As shown by the recent increase in job mobility among Japanese top managers, the example is coming from the top.

In a departure from the past, by means of bonus schemes more directly linked to individual and company performance, abolition of across-the-board, and automatic wage rises, companies intend to keep stable their redistribution ratio of the value-added to the employees in order to always adjust it flexibly to business conditions (Sueki, 2003). But, overall, they declare that a decrease in their labour costs is important but not the highest priority of the changes in the HRM system (*Shukan* Diamondo, 12 June 2004). Rather the message to employees is that it is not possible to maintain a system with automatic wage increases and promotion. Reforms are based on the premise of the existence of a large and diversified external labour market for all kinds of labour. Especially in the case of white collar workers, the external market should no longer be a last resort for employees in trouble. Thanks to employability schemes it should offer the opportunity to the two parties to develop a contingent type of mutual relationship and commitment based on a market-oriented evaluation and remuneration systems. In achieving this objective, companies would at last develop an HRM system on the lines of the one they had wanted to establish just after World War II.

Regular workers in the companies promoting this approach are reminded that they are still key stakeholders and trust remains the basis of the relationship. However, companies cannot be expected to continue to assume welfare corporatist obligations. Companies are all the more encouraged to remove the welfare corporatist schemes such as housing and family-related allowances that employees do not seem to desire to be continued themselves. Canon, for instance, has devoted large resources to informing its young employees about the new HRM system. No paternalistic seniority bias should be expected, but long-term careers in the company will remain the norm for the well-performing regular employees. Meanwhile Takeda Chemicals the corporate culture that the company claims has been created is characterized by 'the strong identity of the self that is sustained by individual judgement and responsibility. Autonomy is a key factor, employees discuss freely and frankly in an organic system where the chain of command and the reporting systems are clear and well understood' (Yanashita, 2001, p. 126).

Better harmonization of job function, performance and reward

Up until recently functional specialization was not a significant factor in wage determination. Most companies would now like to link them more closely, particularly to compensate those in managerial positions but it is expected ultimately to spread to all categories of employees. In the case of *seikashugi*, performance evaluation is supposed (Table 10.2) to be directly linked to monthly pay, whereas under *noryokushugi* pay differentials in the short term could *de facto* only appear in the bonus and special allowances because of the quasi automatic across-the-board yearly wage increase and the willingness to minimize wage differential in the short term. The latent skills not directly linked to a specific job that were taken into consideration in promotion and pay in the grading system ought to be replaced by the obligation to demonstrate their actual use. This is considered all the more necessary by many companies that they recognize that the drift towards seniority has been so strong that the rankings are often no longer credible (Debroux, 2003).

In the case of blue-collar workers real *tanokoka* (polyvalence) and a high level of expertise are still necessary for a number of tasks. What Itagaki (2004, p. 160) called the 'deep extraction of fundamental production technology' allows the adjustment of manufacturing process and equipment in accordance to very fine differences in production facilities and product characteristics, or changes in environmental conditions. It requires knowledge and abilities accumulated on the shop floor and remains the basis of the competitiveness of Japanese companies in cars, but also digital cameras, DVD players and flat panel TVs. The mastering of such skills should be rewarded as in the past in a long-term perspective in taking into account the mastering of the *kaizen* process and the accumulated experience. However it is also acknowledged that many types of skills became irrelevant or obsolete because of business and/or technological changes. For many workers the use of sophisticated equipment and automation make direct involvement in the *kaizen* process less relevant without the specialized knowledge that they cannot be expected to acquire in view of their academic background. In the case of tasks where there is little accumulation of skills and knowledge over time, efficiency-based pay may be more suitable, with only a small part

Table 10.1   Changes to the pay system after 1999 (per cent)

	HR system for management	HR system for non-management
Competency	15.5	18.4
Broadbanding	18.7	21.3
Larger basic pay differential	26.5	28.4
Implementation basic pay decrease system	36.1	27.0
Set minimum/maximum basic pay range	18.7	27.7
Implement merit increase matrix	9.7	11.3
More job/role-based pay	23.9	18.4
More job ability-based pay	11.6	17.7
More individual performance based pay	38.7	29.8
More individual performance-based bonus payout differentiation	47.7	48.9

Source: Romu Gyosei Kenkyujo (2002).

Table 10.2   Recent changes made to the regular wage increase by selected companies

Canon (2002)	Regular wage increase removed; experience element retained for employees under 32 years of age
Honda (2002)	Regular wage increase removed, except for new employees during the first three years
Seiko Epson (2003)	Regular wage increase removed for middle managers and above
Mitsubishi Motors (2003)	Regular wage increase removed; adoption of performance-related pay for all employees
Takeda Chemicals (2003)	Regular wage increase removed; adoption of performance-related pay for all employees

Source: *Nihon Keizai Shimbun*, 13 March 2004.

of the basic wage (still remaining skill- and experience-based and thus indirectly linked to tenure and age (Debroux, 2003)).

There have been moves towards a Japanese-style job-related system (*Nihon Keizai Shimbun*, 13 March 2004), but the basis for remuneration is seldom linked to straight job-related rankings except in the case of specialists whose career is clearly circumscribed. This contrasts with the large increase in the use of the contribution-based system for middle and upper managerial personnel (Debroux, 2003). As for lower-ranking executives and rank-and-file employees a still strong intention to retain the grading system based on skills is noticeable (Sueki, 2003). However the latter is being progressively refined to ensure there is less misallocation of money, time and talent. To alleviate the problem of proliferating ranking categories with ill-defined differentiating criteria, rankings are being grouped into broader bands.

In 2002 Matsushita Electric (Table 10.1) had reached an agreement with its union concerning a dual remuneration system for the rank-and-file employees from the year 2002 onwards. Employees who were in charge of planning and decision-making were paid according to their performance, while those involved in clerical work and manufacturing would be paid according to a mainly seniority-based system. However from April 2004 Matsushita removed the age factor for all employees and announced that automatic wage increases would not be guaranteed anymore to any of them (*Nihon Keizai Shimbun*, 13 March 2004).

Introduction of the concept of competence

Japanese companies wish to develop an evaluation and remuneration system that incorporates behavioural aspects as well as the skills and abilities displayed during the work process. To this end they have become interested in the concept of competency which emphasizes the importance of knowledge, skills, behaviour and attitude, although they are aware that it might lead to rigidity if applied too formally. The company's restructuring process entails rapid changes in the relative importance of departments or given activities inside the organization. The distribution of tasks among the members of groups responsible for projects may change over time with the evolution of the projects. The size of their respective jobs may increase or decrease and it is difficult to define precisely what the optimum behaviour could be (Sueki, 2003). In attempting to select the characteristics of the appropriate response unambiguously, some types of behaviour may be excluded because they are considered useless in acquiring a very specific competence. In doing so, intangible tacit knowledge and the potential, latent aspects of skill and ability are liable to be neglected. That is why many companies combine it with a broad-banding system giving them the opportunity to devote resources to building up skills in the younger employees, while providing for flexibility in job allocation (Debroux, 2003).

By so doing they believe that the concept of competency can be applied effectively and replace the skill-grading system. The new system would not take previous contributions and performance expectations into account, and would be based on demonstration of the actual skills in a specific family of jobs. It would not reward skills that may be obsolete or unnecessary. With enough flexibility in the setting of the job bands and in the appraisal of the results, and with good communication between managers and subordinates, companies are confident that they can create an evaluation and wage system that would not be thwarted again by the seniority element. Competency copes with the demand for employability and allows the recruitment of mid-career managers and specialists under good pay and status conditions. Therefore it does not necessarily assume long-term service in the company. Moreover, whilst facilitating the creation of fast tracks for the most promising young employees, it renders companies free of searching out adequate posts for redundant personnel, which was becoming common in the 1980s and 1990s. If they do not have the necessary competencies they cannot get access to new jobs. None of the elements of competency-based schemes is new to Japanese context. Evaluation based on criteria of leadership capability, skills and knowledge acquisition, attitudes and behaviour were the very basis of the skill-grading system. That is why the competency-based schemes were utilized at the beginning as a way to restructure the latter. However, it is observed that they focus on much more limited job families than before, confirming the move (albeit incomplete) towards more explicitly job-based wage systems (Debroux, 2003).

The use of Management By Objective and annualized schemes

In a survey conducted in 2001, about 80 per cent of the respondents stated that they had adopted a Management By Objective (MBO) scheme (Matsushige, 2002). MBO allows for quantitative evaluation but they seem to be used mainly as tools to establish clearer responsibility and accountability for the job. Projects can take several years and involve staff changes, making it difficult to set objectives and conduct short-term evaluations based on a precise job (Sueki, 2003). Moreover doubts have been expressed about the real intentions of some companies. MBO schemes are often considered as just a new name for what Japanese people call '*norma*' (quantitative and or qualitative standards of performance to be achieved by the worker), with the negative connotation of targets imposed in a top-down manner in sales and manufacturing activities. In this sense it would be a far cry from what the companies envisioned: the development of evaluation and motivational tools in response to employees' desire for individual self-achievement and individual performance evaluation. As in other countries, there is concern that it could lead to employees setting deliberately less challenging targets and developing a short-term orientation (Takahashi, 2004).

On the whole, however, companies seem to be addressing the problem. Even when there is open communication between employees and managers and with active employee participation in target setting, where the definition of success is based on uncertain and changing parameters, the achievement of quantitative targets can only be one of the criteria used to determine wages. The MBO schemes are mainly used for appraisal for the employees' potential, and training and career development purposes (Debroux, 2001).

About 35 per cent of companies with more than 1000 employees claim to have adopted annualization plans. Of these, 85 per cent had only applied it to managers (*Rosei Jiho*, 5 January 2002). Annualization schemes are considered to be a key element of *seikashugi*-type of HRM reforms because they eliminate all the seniority and corporatist welfare factors and allow the creation of a much larger pay differential. Length of tenure is not taken into consideration; automatic annual increase and the quasi totality of allowances disappear. In large companies the annual difference at the section chief level can amount to about 2 million yen. The typical performance-related pay representative of the annualization schemes is a job-based wage in the broad sense. The jobs are no longer linked to status, as in the skill-grading system (Sueki, 2003).

A new evaluation and remuneration system for non-executive personnel

Changes in the evaluation and classification of non-executive personnel, that is those who are members of the in-house union, tend to place emphasis on greater transparency and rationality, delineating job contents, tasks and functions and linking remuneration to the employment structure that emerges from this. The organizational and motivational realities of largely team- and group-oriented company structures are also taken into account. Nevertheless there have been attempts to readopt *dekigatakyu*; that is, the wage system based on individual measured performance for a number of factory jobs. This almost disappeared in the 1950s with mass production and the use of assembly lines which required group work. But nowadays many workers are again working individually or in very small groups to complete an entire product, for example in work cell production or individual work stations. Therefore it is possible to partially reintroduce a kind of efficiency-based wage based on *seikashugi* principles (Sueki, 2003).

Some companies have developed approaches that aim to satisfy the demands of young, promising low-ranking managers. In the operational type of work they perform, the boundaries between jobs are blurred. There is a need for collaboration in crossing these boundaries and team activities must thus be taken into account. Moreover, as a remnant of welfare corporatism, companies remain aware that these young managers are likely to start families and therefore need a stable income. Hence some elements of seniority may be adequate and the skill-grading system is still the most suitable one at their career stage. However to satisfy their demand for recognition of individual merit at the same time, just a few years away from promotion to a managerial position, multiple pay-rate systems are used until they become eligible for future

Table 10.3   Remuneration model based on career stage

	Seniority-based pay	Skill-based pay	Performance-related pay
Non-managerial employees (aged 20–30)	Principal component	Secondary component	Not applicable
Lower manager (aged 30–40)	Secondary component	Principal component	Not applicable
Section head (aged 40–50)	Not applicable	Principal component	Secondary component
Department head (aged 50 plus)	Not applicable	Secondary component	Principal component

Source: Nihon Shakai Keizai Seisansei Honbu (2002).

managerial performance-related pay. Although they may stay in the same ranking they can be put into a different pay rate category each year. The schemes operate as a 'recovery-based' system, meaning that evaluation for a given year has no influence on the rating for the following year. Employees may move from the lowest rate in one year to the highest in the next, with a corresponding differential in their salary. In a later stage of their career, when planning and supervisory tasks start to outweigh operational ones, they will gradually move towards a more job-based, performance evaluation and remuneration system (Table 10.3) (Debroux, 2001).

The development of fair evaluation procedures

Equitable methods of evaluation, remuneration and career development planning are crucial in gaining employees acceptance of the new schemes. Fear for the future, induced by the reforms, is widespread. The social safety net is thin compared to the European welfare states and the loss of one's job may lead to a drastic decline in living standards. Moreover, despite the growth of the external labour market, it is not yet as developed as in Western countries (Sueki, 2003). Therefore, shifting to another company entails a great social and economic risk. So, as employees who receive poor evaluations may receive no promotion or may even be demoted, have generally no choice but to stay in the company, keeping them motivated requires their acceptance of the fairness of the evaluation. Although the seniority-based and skill-grading systems were based on unclear criteria, great efforts were made to ensure that they were understood and accepted by all employees. In the case of the skill-grading system, remuneration was unified at the company level, providing a base of comparison for all employees. If the trend towards distinction by job categories is confirmed, as it is likely to be, an overall internal comparison based on a portfolio of skills, largely usable and comparable all over the company under the traditional grading system will become impossible. As the external market is insufficiently developed to provide objective external benchmarks for each occupation and specialist skill, it means that for the time being both parties will be forced to accept compromises based on the existing traditional rules.

The *seikashugi* systems's bias towards short-term performance has been recognized: employees may concentrate on their own individual performance rather than that of the team or group, to the possible detriment of the organization. They may also refuse to be transferred to jobs where they could suffer under the *seikashugi* approach (Debroux, 2003). They have to be convinced of the fairness of their evaluation, but to establish the exact contribution of jobs where there is little differentiation takes time and represents a heavy burden for line managers. The difference between the previous system and the new one is that the stakes are higher for both appraised and appraisers. A negative evaluation can lead to a lower income, demotion or even loss of employment. Conversely, it may also be negative for the career of the appraiser if it leads to a deterioration of the performance of the employee. That is why precise information to employees regarding their performance evaluation systems from management and HRM departments is so critical (Takahashi, 2004). They must be sure that their employer is providing full information, with them regarding such items as evaluation criteria and procedures, and they should be given the opportunity to discuss their evaluations, receive formal explanations of the results, and possibly have them reconsidered. If such measures are adopted, employees are more likely to perceive the evaluation system as fair and accept the decisions made. As shown in Table 10.4 stating the result of a survey undertaken by Nikkei BP with 120 human resource managers in large Japanese companies listed on the stock exchange first section, the most common complaints made by employees on their performance-related pay system refer to the ambiguities and inconsistencies of the evaluation process.

For the time being, in most Japanese companies, disclosure of the results and the feedback associated with such disclosure are conducted

Table 10.4   Observed negative reactions and issues for performance-based pay system (%)

Non rigorous evaluation standard	74.2
Inconsistent evaluation standard/practice between departments, unfair treatment	68.4
Unfair evaluation/recognition	64.5
More assertive employees tend to get better evaluation	54.5
Focused on own individual objectives only, do not support other/ team members	46.7
Once own objectives exceeded, no more effort made	40.3
Not suited to routine and steady work	31.2
New system can be an excuse for cost reduction	18.5
Set easily achievable objectives	11.1
Volatility in income makes it harder to plan private life	8.4

Source: *Nikkei BP*, Survey for 120 HR Managers, April 2001.

in meetings between the employees and their supervisors. Few companies have a formal system of disclosure. Similarly formal mechanisms for handling appeals against the evaluation results and for responding to complaints have been developed by a relatively small percentage of companies (Sueki, 2003).

Job classification and *seikashugi*

In order to introduce the *seikashugi* system it is necessary to change recruitment practices and job structures. More than 50 per cent of large companies with more than 3000 workers are said to have a multiple track system arranged by job category (Sueki, 2003). This is not new as it reflects the traditional differentiation by academic credential and assignment to specific job categories according to that credential. However, so far most companies have continued to use a common wage curve table for all employees. In all of them the rules for promotion and the appraisal criteria have always differed according to the track. But it had not been translated so far into the adoption of clear and distinct multiple wage curves by job families, leading to ambiguity in the wage setting. This approach reflected the traditional preference for taking a company-wide approach to a whole range of human resource issues. From now on, it may be more difficult to keep it in organizations with employees having diverse specialized skills, different career expectations and patterns of promotion and professional values. So, with the systematization of multiple career tracks resulting from the use of diversified categories of worker, it can be expected that a multiple wage curve system can be developed. If sufficient basic differences among the tracks are formulated, homogeneous treatment may be maintained within the different tracks with an accepted salary and career structure. To the extent that the dispatch to a given track is made according to fair criteria (does not discriminate according to gender or age, for instance) it may help to create homogeneity under diversity and solve to some extent the difficulty in reconciling workers with different approaches to motivation and career expectations.

With the enlargement of the external labour market, market rates are likely to emerge for all types of job, making adjustment of the internal wage-setting process less necessary. A number of large companies are recruiting on this basis in order to satisfy the demand by young graduates' for early specialization, and unions are also starting to think in these terms. Denki Rengo, a leading member of the largest union confederation, Rengo, decided to replace the existing method of determining wages with a system of categorizing wages by type of occupation. The aim of this system is to improve the wage for each occupational category, and to apply the same wage level throughout the industry. An intra-industry minimum wage, below which workers should not accept a position, will be established for all occupations. Any amount above that level will be negotiable (*Asahi Shimbun*, 4 July 2002). Determining pay in this way will facilitate worker mobility and act as a sort of safety net. The unions expect that once the system takes hold it will strengthen their bargaining position. Similar moves are being made by other industry unions. For example the Confederation of Japan Automobile Workers' Unions, has decided to abandon its conventional demand for cost-of-living wage rises and focus more on wage increases by occupational type and skill (ibid., 4 July 2002).

Conclusion

The pace of HRM-related reforms has accelerated since the mid 1990s. The traditional system, based on corporate welfare, is now perceived as so flawed and outdated that it can never again meet the needs of both companies and employees. However companies often complain about the problems the reforms have generated, such as reduced motivation and increased staff turnover (Takahashi, 2004). Many of them decided to downgrade the traditional ties they had with their employees during the long crisis period. In that respect, *seikashugi* concepts in a narrow sense were (and still are) indeed widely used as a labour costs control policy. Therefore for a good number of employees *seikashugi* is perceived to lead to deteriorating working condition in terms of both remuneration and employment stability. While elite employees will be increasingly motivated by favourable incentive measures. The rest of the regular employees are likely to experience stricter limits on pay. In many cases even a decline in real pay might be unavoidable. So even if employment tenure is preserved, which is far from assured, a growing number of employees may be compelled to accept a lesser job. This makes it essential to develop sensible policies to motivate employees with limited career expectations. If companies just tell employees that they have to take responsibility for their own careers without providing the means for them to do so, for example on-the-job and off-the-job training programmes, the consequences are likely to be negative. It is argued that employees need both company-specific skills and general skills to give them a sense of purpose in their activities, the feeling that their future is reasonably secure and, if this is not the case, that they will be in a good position to find another job with good conditions. Advocacy of the employability concept will credit distrust if it does not satisfy those two conditions. Employees can only be expected to become really responsible for their own skills and knowledge as requested by their employers if they receive enough information from the companies and the public authorities, and enough opportunity and time to learn what they deem will be profitable for them. Although initiatives are being taken by public authorities, leading companies and business organizations, most of them remain cautious about introducing new schemes in a period of business uncertainty (Fujimura, 2004).

Trying to introduce it through contribution or competency schemes for jobs with small differentials could be very costly and cumbersome for many companies, especially smaller ones. That is why it has even been suggested that elements of seniority be introduced again for some categories of personnel (Takahashi, 2004). Likewise, multiple tracks and distinction by job category may offer advantages to both parties, as shown by the initiatives taken by the union federations. However if they become a source of discrimination against some groups, for instance, female employees, the backlash could be very detrimental to the organizations. Doubt can also be expressed about the strong emphasis put on large differentials in monetary reward in the new motivational tools linked to *seikashugi*. This reflects the strongly ingrained idea that employees always give priority to money and fast promotion. However in view of the fact that many people are giving greater priority to the quality of their lives in general, more and more employees are favouring job content and private life over money and fast promotion. This calls for more imaginative policies to satisfy those workers who are looking at their career in this way. Even for managerial class personnel it is not possible to create rules that cover every case. On the contrary, this could be very counterproductive. Therefore schemes that allow for diversity become all the more important.

Finally, it is necessary to find a glue that will bind companies and employees together in the long term. Obviously in the present environment there are fewer compelling reasons for both parties to stick to long-term binding commitments. *Seikashugi* gives greater flexibility to both parties, but it is bound to lower the level of mutual trust and of employee involvement in the long-term well-being of the organization. If they were to think that they were merely considered as expendable resources, with the exception of a small protected group of high flyers, it is unlikely that they would devote as much energy and dedication to the company. Regular employees have never thought they had gained the right to a free ride. Rather they always believed that they also had obligations to the company and that top managers too had a duty to do their best. Therefore not only have their high level of skills helped companies to be competitive, but also the long-term commitment that has been created has served as a mutual control on behaviour. In that sense the dedication of the employees to the organization has played a very important role in terms of internal management discipline. This is a precious asset that companies should try to preserve. What was called the 'community of fate' symbolizing the strong relationships existing in Japanese organizations, is probably dead. The younger generation of employees wish to have more contingent relationships with their company. But they largely remain attached to the development of a stable career. Therefore should companies decide to develop policies that combine more market-oriented business practices associated with the discipline of the capital market with traditional elements of their traditional HRM system, the support of all employees will be needed to make this a success.

References

Abegglen, J. C. (1958) *The Japanese Factory: Aspects of its Social Organization* (Glencoe, Ill.: The Free Press).

Debroux, P. (2003) Human Resource Management in Japan: A Time of Uncertainties (Aldershot: Ashgate).

Denki Rengo Research Institute (2001) *Chosa Jiho: Denki Sangyo no Koyo Kozo ni Kansuru Chosa*, no. 323 (Survey of the Employment Structure in the Electric Industry) (Tokyo: Denki Rengo).

Fujimura, H. (2004) 'Managing the Development of One's Own Vocational skills in Japanese Companies', *Japan Labour Review*, 1 (3), pp. 5–6.

Fukutani, M. (2003) 'Historical Analysis and Ongoing Change of the Personnel Evaluation System', *Nihon Keiei Shindan Gakkai Ronshu*, 3, pp. 13–26.

Hart, R. and S. Kawasaki (1999) *Work and Pay in Japan* (Oxford: Oxford University Press).

Hazama, H. (1997) *The History of Labour Management in Japan* (London: Macmillan).

Itagaki, H. (2004) Characteristics and Future of the Japanese Corporate Management System, paper presented at the Euro-Asia Management Studies Association Annual Conference, Hong Kong, 3–6 November.

Keizai Doyukai (1994, 1999) *Dai 14 kai Kigyo Hakusho 'Ko' no Kyoso Ryoku Kojo ni Yoru Nihon Kigyo no Saisei Keieisha no Noryoku ga Towareru Jidai* (Fourteenth Company White Paper: A Period When Managers' Capability Should be Challenged in Order to Transform, Japanese Companies Thanks to the Development of Individual Capabilities) (Tokyo: Keizai Doyukai).

Kinoshita, T. (2001) Chingin Seido no Tenkan to Seikashugi Chingin no Mondaiten (The Conversion of the Wage and Personnel System and the Issue of the Result Principle Wages), *Annual Review of Labour Sociology*, 12 (November), pp. 55–72.

Kokura, M. (1999) *Kokura REP Keiei Gaku* (Kokura's Management Theory) (Tokyo: Nikkei BP sha).

Koshiro, K. (2000) *A Fifty Year History of Industry and Labor in Postwar Japan*, (Tokyo: Japan Institute of Labour).

Magota, R. (1970) *Nenko-Chingin no Ayumi to Mirai- Chingin Taikei 100 Nen-shi* (The Past and Future of the Seniority Wage System – 100 years of the Japanese wage system), (Sangyo R Chosa-sho).

Matsushige, H. (2002) 'Seikashugi to wa nanide, honto ni Koka ga aru no ka?' (What is the meaning of seikashugi, does it really work?), *Nihon Rodo Kenkyu Zasshi*, 501 (April), pp. 75–6.

Miyauchi, Y. (2001) *Miyauchi Keieiron* K. Miyauchi's (Management Theory) (Tokyo: Tôkyô Keizai Shimposha).

Nihon Shakai Keizai Seisansei Honbu (2001) *Nenpan Nihonteki Jinji Seido no Genjo to Kadai, Nihon Shakai Keizai Seisansei Honbu Jinjiiin, 2001, Noryoku, Jisseki nado no Hyoka. Katsuyo ni Kansuru Kenkyukai Saishu Hokoku* (Current Situation and Topics Concerning Japanese-Style Human Resource Management, Yearbook of the Human Resource Committee, 2001, Final Report of the Study Group on Competence, Appraisal of Performance) (Tokyo: Nihon Shakai Keizai Seisansei Honbu).

Nikkei BP (2002) *Survey of HR managers* (Tokyo: Nikkei BP).

Nikkeiren (1969), *Noryokushugi Kanri, Sono Riron to Jissen* (Performance Management, Theory and Practice) (Tokyo: Nikkeiren Shuppanbu).

Nikkeiren (1995) *Nihonteki Keiei no Shin-jidai* (A New Era for Japanese-Style Management) (Tokyo: Nikkeiren Shuppanbu).

Okuda, H. (2001) *Nihon Rodo Nenkan* (Japan Labour Yearbook) (Ohara Shakai Mondai Kenkyujo, Hosei University), pp. 123–4.

Rengo (2001) *Rengo Hakusho* (Rengo White Book) (Tokyo: Rengo).

Romu Gyosei Kenkyujo (1999) *Koyo Kanri no Jitsumu* (Practice of Employment Management) (Tokyo: Rodosho Seisaku Chosabu).

Romu Gyosei Kenkyujo (2002) 'Survey on the Pay System Change', *Rosei Jiho*, 5 (January) pp. 18–23.

Sueki, N. (2003) *Shigoto Base Chingin no Sekkei* (Devising the Work-Based Wage) (Tokyo: Shakai Keizai Seisansei Honbu, Seisansei Rodo Joho Center).

Takahashi, N. (2004) *Kyomo Seikashugi* (Impossible seikashugi) (Tokyo: Nikkei BP sha).

Tokai Sogo Kenkyujo (2001) *Jinji Seido no Genjo to Kongo no Kaizen no Hokosei* (Present Situation of the Human Resource Management System and the Directions of Change) (Tokai Sogo Kenkyujo).

Yanashita, K. (2001) *Wakariyasui Jinji ga Kaisha o Kaeru* (Simple HRM Can Change a Company) (Tokyo: Nihon Keizai Shimbunsha).

11
Employee Control of Working Time: International Comparisons[1]

Peter Berg, Eileen Appelbaum, Tom Bailey and Arne L. Kalleberg

Working arrangements that reflect employers' requirement for greater flexibility and employees' desire for job security and a better balance between work and private life are changing today's workplaces. Flexible working arrangements such as part-time work, teleworking, compressed working weeks, contracts that specify annual working hours and time banks have increased substantially since 1990 in the advanced industrial economies (Bettio *et al.*, 1998). While these arrangements are often seen as a way of increasing flexibility for employers and employees alike, the extent to which they benefit the latter depends on the degree to which employees have control over their working time.

Despite the growing importance of flexibility policies and practices there has been relatively little research on firms' reasons for adopting them. Nor have there been comparative studies of the tension between employer and employee control across countries. The purpose of this chapter is to provide a foundation for the development of public policy and private practice by comparing employee control over working time in four countries, including Japan.

We begin by briefly discussing the drivers of change in working time and then identify three factors that affect employees' control of working time across countries. Next, using cases from individual countries we illustrate how these factors actually affect working time and employees' control over it. We then focus on how these factors affect employee control over working time in Japan.

International developments in working time

Working time has been central focus of policy initiatives and collective bargaining in the European Union (EU), Australia and Japan since the early 1990s. In Japan the discussion of flexible working time has been framed in terms of what constitutes a comfortable lifestyle (Imada, 1997). The Japanese do not feel rich, Imada argues, because the overemphasis on work and long hours has made it difficult for many Japanese to enjoy family life. The balance between work and private life has become a matter for public policy because of Japan's low birth rate and ageing population and the government's desire to increase women's participation in paid employment.[2] The persistence of unemployment and the sluggish economy have led Japanese companies and policy makers to introduce greater flexibility, including more flexible work schedules, as a means of revitalizing the workplace and the economy (JIL, 2000).

In the EU and Australia, changes in working time are largely driven by employers' need to match work schedules to variations in the demand for labour and employees' interest in protecting or creating jobs. Collective bargaining in Germany, Italy and Australia has frequently led to reduced working hours at the enterprise level while providing employers with greater flexibility in scheduling work by such means as annualized hours of work, time bank schemes, individual working time contracts, and flexible starting and finishing times (Bettio *et al.*, 1998).

In the United States working hours increased in the 1980s and 1990s, to the point where US workers now work more hours than workers in any other industrialized country – on average 1978 hours per year (ILO, 1999, 2001). Middle-class parents in dual-income households worked a total of 3932 hours in 2000, more than the hours worked in two full-time jobs in most European countries (Mishel *et al.*, 2003). As a result of employers' pursuit of greater workplace flexibility and employees' interest in balancing work and family responsibilities, the way work is accomplished and scheduled is changing. The standard 40-hour week is disappearing in many occupations: managers and professionals regularly put in extra hours to meet deadlines and many employees who are paid by the hour are required to work overtime or evening hours (Golden and Figart, 2000; Golden, 2001). Often the trade-off for managers and professionals is greater control over when and where work takes place, as reflected in the growth of flexible starting and finishing times and teleworking (Appelbaum and Golden, 2002). For many US workers, however, the need for flexibility and control over working time means accepting part-time or contingent working arrangements.

Explaining variations in employees' control over working time

Working time has two main dimensions: duration of work and timing of work. Control over the duration of working hours concerns the established daily, weekly, or annual hours of work and whether one has the ability to increase or decrease those hours. This type of control is often reflected in the taking of part-time jobs or reducing the hours worked in a full-time job. Control over the timing of work refers to the time at which work is performed during the day or week. These two dimensions define the work schedule; thus, we define employee control over working time as the ability of individuals to alter their work schedule. Total control refers to the situation in which employees work whatever schedule they like and can change it at will. Total lack of control refers to the situation in which the employer can unilaterally change the day–hour combination. Actual arrangements usually lie somewhere between these two extremes.

Three broad factors affect the degree of control individuals have over working time: the institutional environment in the country in question, labour market conditions, and management and union strategies. Figure 11.1 outlines the relationship between these factors and employees' control over working time.

Employment relations institutions play a key part in determining the relative bargaining power of employers and employees over the control

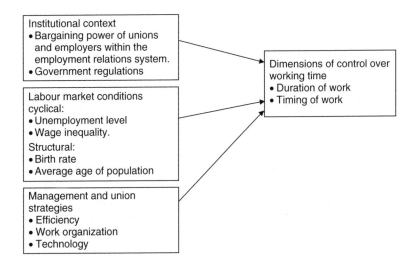

Figure 11.1   Framework for examining control over working time

of working time. The strength of unions and their position in the employment relations system determine their ability to negotiate work schedules that benefit employees. Strong unions or works councils monitor working time at the establishment level and ensure that workers who have accrued paid time off can take it when they need it. Individuals' control over working time is increased when collective agreements enable them to choose from a variety of working time options to suit their needs. Conversely when employers exclusively determine when employees can take time off or are required to work overtime, employees' control over working time is restricted.

Government regulations also affect control over working time by limiting evening and weekend work and fixing maximum daily, weekly or annual working hours. Moreover laws on shop-closing hours, particularly in Europe, restrict the scheduling options available to shop workers, especially those who may want to increase their hours.

Labour market conditions vary from country to country and directly affect the relative bargaining power of employers and employees. We divide these conditions into cyclical and structural factors. If unemployment is low there may be an excess demand for certain types of employees, giving them greater bargaining power over working hours or work schedules. This is particularly relevant for white-collar professionals as there is less standardization of working time, and it enables unions to negotiate collective control over working time. In addition increased wage inequality in the labour market and slow wage growth may prompt those at the low end of the labour market to increase their hours in order to improve their income. Structural factors such as the birth rate and the average age of the population can also affect labour market dynamics and public policy on working time. In countries with a low birth rate and an ageing labour force, governments often introduce policies to support increased personal and parental leave and flexible work schedules so that women can combine work with motherhood. An ageing population can also result in skill shortages in the labour market, which can influence employees' bargaining power.

Management strategies also affect the structure of working time and employees' control over it. In response to competition firms may adjust working time in order to lower costs or improve efficiency, for instance by matching working hours to demand. In addition management and unions may negotiate certain types of work schedules to workers greater autonomy. For example organizing workers into groups or teams with some autonomy and decision-making power is sometimes linked to the ability of groups or individuals to schedule their own working time (Lehndorff, 2000). Also, integrating digital technologies into the work process can lead to more flexible working arrangements and improve employee control. Technologies such as mobile phones, pagers, email and computers can give workers greater control over the location and timing of work. However they may also cause employers to expect employees to be available to deal with work matters at all times.

These three factors – institutional environment, labour market conditions and management and union strategies – vary from country to country. In countries where there is less government regulation of the labour market and weak collective bargaining institutions, competition in the labour market may limit the degree of employee control over working time and give managers more power to shape working time. In tight labour markets we would expect workers with skills that are in high demand to be more successful in negotiating work schedules that suit their needs, but at the same time overall employee control over working time would be low in all occupational groups.

Conversely, where there is more government regulation of the labour market and strong collective bargaining institutions, the effect of competitive labour market conditions to increase the power of employees to negotiate work schedules would be diminished. More uniform, collectively negotiated working time would apply to all workers in a firm or industry. In addition government regulation of working time might give individuals the right to demand reduced hours or alternative work schedules.

Cross-national differences in employee control over working time

This section draws on field studies we conducted in Germany, Sweden, the Netherlands, Italy, Japan, Australia and the United States during the summer and autumn of 2000. In each of these countries we visited companies and hospitals, and spoke to government officials, academic experts, unions, employers' associations, managers and workers' representatives about work and family policies and practices, including working time. In all we conducted 208 interviews, 184 of them outside the United States. Here we shall limit our discussion to the four countries that best illustrate the effect of the three factors discussed above on employee control over working time.

Before we begin we shall briefly consider policies of the European Union (EU) that have had a profound effect on labour and working time across the EU. Through the use of directives, the EU has set guidelines for working time and working arrangements throughout the EU. For example a 1993 EU directive encouraged greater flexibility in working time and set standards for annual paid leave and average weekly working hours, and a 1997 directive required equal treatment for full- and part-time workers. In contrast to the other countries in our study, in the EU workers are treated as stakeholders in the firm. This is reflected in high union membership in most EU countries, the importance given to collective bargaining in the workplace, and various forms of legally mandated employee participation across the EU.

The latter situation contrasts with that in the United States, where the property rights of individuals and corporations are given much greater weight in corporate law and governance. Moreover the control of unions over working time is much weaker and union membership is much lower: about 13.5 per cent of the workforce compared with an average of 30.4 per cent in the EU (Carley, 2001). In addition employees have no legal right to participate in workplace decisions, although this may be granted by the employer or won in collective bargaining. We shall now look at the situation in the four selected countries.

The Netherlands

In consultation with unions and employers, the government of the Netherlands has passed several laws to make working time more flexible and give individuals greater choice over their working hours. The Working Time Act of 1996 has norms for working time but allowed firms to deviate from these norms by collective agreement. This has encouraged innovation in the schedules of full-time jobs. New practices include working time accounts, annual hours of work contracts, sabbatical leave, part-time work, job sharing and 35- or 36-hour working weeks.

For example in 1997 the chemical firm AKZO-Nobel and its various unions negotiated an agreement for employees to have an additional eight days' annual leave, to be taken at the employee's discretion. Workers are free to 'sell' these days back to AKZO-Nobel in exchange for a wage increase of 3.2 per cent. Alternatively they can allow AKZO-Nobel to decide on the timing of their extra days off, in return for which they receive another four days off (12 in total), so end up working a 36-hour week on average (European Industrial Relations Observatory, 1997).

In 1999 the Dutch social partners reached agreement on a framework for further individualization of the terms of employment. This agreement allows unions and employers to designate a number of benefits that can be exchanged for each other. For example, the retail firm KBB allows employees to exchange holidays and bonus pay for other types of leave, additional pay or subsidies for child care expenses (van het Kaar, 1999). These arrangements demonstrate that it is possible through collective bargaining to deal with some of the difficult trade-offs that occur when making working time more flexible. Workers who prefer to work more and earn more are able to do so, while those who prefer to work less are able to benefit from working time reductions.

Perhaps the best-known consequence of the more flexible working hours in the Netherlands is the increase of part-time jobs. There is a stronger preference for part-time work on the part of both men and women in the Netherlands than in other countries. In 1998, 18 per cent of employed males and 68 per cent of employed females worked part-time, compared with the EU average of 6 per cent and 33 per cent respectively (Nickell and Van Ours, 2000).

The promotion of part-time work began in the 1980s as a measure to create jobs and reduce unemployment. In the tight labour market of the 1990s, however, it functioned to match labour demand and supply. As well as giving employers greater flexibility, it expanded the pool of workers from which employers could recruit and helped employees to achieve a better balance between work and private life.

Two laws regulate part-time work in the Netherlands. First, the Equal Treatment Act of 1993 specifies that part-time workers must be treated the same as full-time workers. This means that part-time employees receive comparable *pro rata* wages, benefits and training opportunities to those received by full-time employees. The Act reflected collective bargaining agreements reached prior to its passage and foreran the 1997 EU directive on the equal treatment of part-time and full-time workers. Second, the Adjustment of Hours Act (also referred to as the Part-Time Employment Act) of 2000 provides workers with the legal right periodically to request reductions of or increases in their weekly working hours. This right is mainly exercised by workers with full-time jobs (rarely mothers) who want to reduce their hours. Unless the employer can provide a valid business reason why this is not possible, the employer is required to honour the request. The law was passed despite the objection of employers, but the latter had been able to win some concessions. For example they can refuse to allow part-time work if they can prove that honouring the request will create a severe problem for the company. In addition employers with 10 or fewer employees are exempt from the law.

The Equal Treatment Act provides part-time workers with some protection against low-quality and low-wage jobs, while the Part-Time

Employment Act provides workers, primarily those in full-time jobs, with the opportunity to exercise control over the duration of their working hours. However it does not address the timing of work, which in principle employers still control.

The United States

The institutional arrangements in the United States are such that workers have little right to reduce their working hours or gain flexibility over their working time. For the vast majority of workers, the most common means of obtaining control over working time is to take part-time or temporary jobs with reduced hours. However there are no legal restrictions against the unequal treatment of part-time and full-time workers in the United States, and these jobs tend to be poorly paid and offer fewer benefits. Half of all part-time jobs in the United States are found in just a handful of industries, most of which pay relatively low wages (Wenger, 2001). In addition to part-time or temporary jobs, workers can seek out companies that offer more flexible schedules that fit their needs. However even in organizations where flexible work arrangements exist as company policy, employees' ability to use them usually depends on the willingness of supervisors to grant flexi time, reduced hours, or telework options to employees (Rapoport and Bailyn, 1996).

In the absence of specific employment laws, the ability of employees to secure flexible working arrangements is largely dependent on the demand for their individual skills in the labour market or their particular value to the employer. This was made clear at a US financial services company where we conducted a series of interviews with managers and employees. This non-union company employed 560 people, mostly professionals, including programmers, data analysts and sales associates. The company offered a benefit package to attract young people and commit them to company. The benefits included four weeks' paid maternity/paternity leave, flexi time, discounts on health club membership, stock options and a paid sabbatical of six months every four years. The average employee worked a 45-hour week. Although employees could reduce their weekly hours to 30 and still retain their benefits, less than 1 per cent worked less than full-time or as temporaries or teleworkers. Because there was no formal company policy on flexibility, the ability of employees to work fewer hours or telecommute depended on the willingness of individual supervisors to approve such an arrangement. Our interviews with employees revealed that only senior employees (those who had worked for the company for more than five years) who had proven their ability to be productive were likely to receive approval for part-time work or telework. Those women who were working less than full-time or were teleworking had had to work hard to convince their managers that they could still get the job done.

Germany

In 1984 the German metalworkers' union (IG Metall) successfully negotiated a reduction in the standard working week. The union viewed this as a job creation strategy in that reducing the time worked by individual workers would force companies to take on additional workers in order to maintain production (for debates on this subject see Layard *et al.*, 1991; Seifert, 1993; Hunt, 1996; Stiller and Zwiener, 1997; Hartog, 1999).

The repercussions of the agreement in the metalworking industry were significant. Negotiations on working time reduction spread to other industries, and this prompted employers to consider working time as a means to gain workplace flexibility in exchange for job growth or, in most cases, to safeguard employment (Seifert, 2000). Throughout the late 1980s and 1990s the adjustment of working time was a source of flexibility for employers and a means of balancing work and personal life for employees.

One of the most widespread forms of flexible working in Germany is the working time account. This allows employees to accrue paid time off in return for working additional hours during periods of high demand. The number of hours accrued depends on the duration of the average working week and whether a premium is attached to the excess hours worked. If the average working week is 35 hours and all hours over 38 per week are banked at a premium rate, a substantial number of hours can be accrued by working a 40-hour week. This contrasts with the accrual of excess hours in countries or industries where the standard working week is 40 hours.

In Germany in 2000, 78 per cent of all private sector establishments offered some form of working time account to their employees. For example 34 per cent combined a working time account and variable working hours linked to fluctuations in demand. In the metalworking industry, 23 per cent of establishments have introduced medium or long-term working time accounts, and flexible working time has become the norm in the industry (Promberger, 2001).

The most famous example of the flexible working week is that at Volkswagen, where in 1993 IG Metall negotiated a standard working week of 28.8 hours in a successful effort to save jobs. When demand is weak, workers may work four eight-hour days for nine weeks and have the tenth week off. This results in an average of 28.8 hours per week over the 10-week period, and workers are paid for that number of hours each week. When demand is strong the company may require workers to work nine 40-hour weeks and again take the tenth week off, resulting in an average 36-hour week. Hours above 28.8 are credited to the employee's working time account and hours above 35 are banked at a premium rate. During slack periods, employees can draw down these accounts and take time off. Alternatively they can exchange the hours for additional pay at the end of the year. They also have the option of transferring the hours to a medium-term or long-term account for longer periods of leave.[3]

As flexible working weeks are negotiated by sector or in individual plants by agreement between labour and management there is great variation in these arrangements. For example the period over which the working week is averaged can be anywhere between three months and a year. The extent to which employees have control over their working time accounts also varies. Some contracts state that workers have the right to take the time off, whereas others specify that employees' wishes for time off will be considered (Bispinck, 1998). There is evidence that some employees use their working time accounts to alter their working week or take time off to deal with personal or family matters (Promberger, 2001; Seifert, 2003).

Japan

Because of its ageing population and declining birth rate, Japan has a strong interest in increasing female participation in the labour force (Goto, 2001). Therefore the government has implemented policies to encourage flexible working time, thus enabling women to combine motherhood and employment. Amendments to the Labour Standards Law in the first half of the 1990s introduced two innovations for full-time employees: the discretionary work scheme and the averaging of weekly working hours.

The discretionary work scheme has modified the method of calculating the number of hours worked by white-collar professionals engaged in 'discretionary work' (Araki, 1996). Such schemes require the consent of individual workers and the support of a joint worker-management committee.

Our survey of a publishing and educational resource company in Tokyo, provides an example of how the discretionary work scheme functions in practice. The 'super-flexitime' scheme at this company was introduced in 1994 and provides workers with control over their schedules. Employees are free to choose their own daily working hours between 7 am and 10 pm as long as they work the required number of hours per month.

However in general the discretionary work scheme has not been widely adopted by companies. In 2002 only 2.1 per cent of enterprises had such a scheme, up from 1.4 per cent in 1997 (JIL, 2003). Similarly regular flexitime has not become widespread, although it is more prevalent in large enterprises. In 2002 only 5 per cent of all enterprises had flexitime but 33 per cent of enterprises with 1000 or more employees offered flexitime. These numbers were slightly lower than the 1999 figures of 5.7 per cent and 36 per cent respectively (ibid.).

The amendments to the Labour Standards Law in 1994 allowed employers to average working hours to a maximum of 52 hours per week and 10 hours a day over a period no longer than a year. The employer is required to formalize this working arrangement by agreement with a union or other worker representative group (Yamakawa, 1998). While individual employees have the right to opt out of this arrangement few have resisted their employer's demands, particularly during times of high unemployment. In 2002 about 43 per cent of all enterprises were averaging the weekly working hours on an annual basis and 15 per cent on a monthly basis. This affected 43 per cent of the workforce (JIL, 2003).

Unlike in Europe, the Japanese annual and monthly working hour schemes are not associated with reduced hours. Over half of Japanese employees aged 20–50 work 45–60 hours per week. Averaging the working week gives the employer more control over working time. Employees can be made to work up to 52 hours a week without higher overtime pay. Moreover the longer the averaging period the longer employees can be made to work the maximum number of weekly hours and the longer they have to wait to take their paid time off. Large companies with strong enterprise unions tend to have shorter averaging periods than smaller companies (ibid.).

Another recent development in Japan is the spread of non-standard forms of employment. For example the proportion of part-time and temporary (agency) workers rose from 21 per cent in 1995 to 26 per cent in 2000 (Sato, 2001). Some people choose part-time or temporary work for the convenience and the shorter hours, especially young unmarried males (about half of whom are students), married women and older workers. However for other workers, primarily female temporary workers and young, single, female part-timers, non-standard employment is the only option if they cannot secure regular employment (ibid.). Unlike in the EU, part-time and temporary workers in Japan are not legally entitled to the same promotion and training opportunities as regular employees.

Conclusion

While control over the duration and timing of work remains largely in managements' hands, employees in certain countries have gained some control over their working time, either through collective bargaining, government legislation or favourable labour market conditions. The precise situation varies from country to country. In EU countries with extensive collective bargaining and high union membership, employees enjoy increased collective control over working time. This collective control is particularly evident in Germany and the Netherlands, where unions and works councils have negotiated reductions in working time and changes to the structure of working time. In some cases collective bargaining has also increased the power of individuals to choose between reduced hours or more income. However even in countries with strong labour representation employers have managed to negotiate flexible working time to their advantage in terms of adjusting labour supply to demand and reducing or eliminating premium overtime pay. While employees may have a say in scheduling through their union or works council representatives, supervisors and department managers maintain the right to approve or veto schedules and paid time off. In short employment relations bodies in the EU have played a key role in increasing the flexibility of working time and monitoring the administration of working time accounts by employers; but employers still have control over the structure of working time and the timing of employees' paid leave.

In the United States, where collective bargaining in the private sector is much less common and labour institutions are weak, employees rely largely on their status in the labour market or their value to a particular employer to gain bargaining power and control over working time. This power, however, is unequally distributed across occupations and is very fleeting since labour market conditions change regularly. Professionals with valuable skills have relatively more control over working time and more flexibility than less skilled workers.

In Japan company unions are weak and government policy is not strictly enforced, so employers are relatively free to structure working time to their interests and employees have little choice but to comply. Moreover, where employers drive the structure of working time, the distribution of flexible forms of working time tends to be narrow, reflecting employer interests. This serves to restrict employee choice of various flexible work schedules and employee control over working time. The growth of non-standard employment arrangements, such as temporary and part-time work, has provided employers with greater flexibility and workers with more options, especially female workers, but such workers have little or no control over their working time. Employees of companies that have introduced discretionary work schemes or the averaging of weekly hours have gained some flexibility, but control over working time remains in the hands of employers. If flexible working time arrangements are to benefit employees as well as employers, policy makers and unions must pay more attention to the issue of control over working time.

Notes

1. A longer version of this chapter was published in the *Industrial and Labor Relations Review* in April 2004. We would like to thank the Alfred P. Sloan Foundation for its generous support of our research. We would also like to thank Karen Markel and Yukari Matsuzuki for excellent research contributions.
2. Women make up 40 per cent of the workforce in Japan and 57 per cent of female employees are married (JIWE, 1999). The proportion of dual-income households and single-parent families is increasing in Japan as elsewhere, and workers need more flexible schedules and greater control over working time in order to balance work with care of children and the elderly (Sato, 2000).
3. Volkswagen has negotiated a set of agreements with IG Metall for its new subsidiary: Auto 5000 GmbH. The workers at this company work under a different set of conditions and receive lower pay than other workers at Volkswagen. The annual average working time for all employees is 35 hours per week, which is the collectively agreed weekly working time in the metalworking industry. The maximum working week is 42 hours and working time accounts have been set up for each employee. If certain shifts are unable to meet their product and quality targets the employees are obliged to work overtime, but the extra hours are only paid if the performance shortfall is the responsibility of the employer. This agreement has essentially created a two-tier employment system at Volkswagen (Schulten, 2001).

References

Appelbaum, E. and L. Golden (2002) *The Standard Work Day or the Highway: Employers Stall in Delivery of More Flexible Arrangements* (Washington, DC: Center for Designing Work Wisely).

Araki, T. (1996) 'Regulation of Working Hours for White-Collar Workers Engaging in Discretionary Activities,' *Japanese Labour Bulletin*, 35 (7).

Bettio, F., E. Del Bono and M. Smith (1998) *Working Time Patterns in the European Union: Policies and Innovations from a Gender Perspective* (Geneva: European Commission).

Bispinck, R. (1998) *Information zur Tarifpolitik, Elemente qualitativer Tarifpolitik Nr. 35, Zwischen Plus und Minus: Zeitkonten in Tarifverträgen* (Dusseldorf: Wirtschafts- und Sozialwissenschaftliches Institut).

Carley, M. (2001) *Industrial Relations in the EU, Japan, and the USA* 2000 (European Industrial Relations Observatory, www.eiro.evrofound.ie).

European Industrial Relations Observatory (1997) *Agreement between AKZO-Nobel and the Unions* (www.eiro.eurofound.ie/print/1997/04/inbrief/NL970411N.html).

Golden, L. (2001) 'Flexible Work Schedules: Which Workers Get Them?', *American Behavioral Scientist*, 44 (7), pp. 1157–78.

Golden, L. and D. M. Figart (2000) *Working Time: International Trends, Theory and Policy Perspectives* (London: Routledge).

Goto, J. (2001) 'Aging Society and the Labor Market in Japan: Should the Fertility Rate be Raised Now? – NO!', *Japanese Labour Bulletin*, 40 (9).

Hartog, J. (1999) *The Netherlands: So What's So Special about the Dutch Model?* International Labour Organization (www.ilo.org/public/english/employment/strat/pub/etp54.htm).

Hunt, J. (1996) *Has Work-Sharing Worked in Germany?* (Cambridge, Mass.: NBER).

ILO (1999) *Key Indicators of the Labour Market* (Geneva: International Labour Organization).

ILO (2001) *Key Indicators of the Labour Market 2001–2002* (Geneva: International Labour Organization).

Imada, S. (1997) *Work and Family Life* (Japan Institute of Labour, www.jil.go.jp/bulletin/year/1997/vol36-08/06.htm).

Japan Institute of Labour (JIL) (2000) *1999 White Paper on the National Lifestyle* (Tokyo: Japan Institute of Labour).

Japan Institute of Labour (JIL) (2003) *Japanese Working Life Profile: 2000 Labour Statistics* (Tokyo: Japan Institute of Labour).

JIWE (1999) *Working Women in Japan* (Tokyo: Japan Institute of Workers' Evolution).

Layard, R., S. Nickell and R. Jackman (1991) *Unemployment: Macroeconomic Performance and the Labour Market* (Oxford: Oxford University Press).

Lehndorff, S. (2000) 'Tertiarization, Work Organization and Working-Time Regulation', Paper presented at the International Conference on The Economics and Socioeconomics of Services: International Perspectives', Lille-Roubqix, 22–23 June.

Mishel, L., J. Bernstein and H. Boushey (2003) *State of Working America, 2002–2003* (Ithaca, NY: Cornell University Press).

Nickell, S. and J. Ours (2000) 'The Netherlands and the United Kingdom: a European Unemployment Miracle?', *Economic Policy*, 30 (April), pp. 137–80.

Promberger, M. (2001) 'Industriebeschäftigte in hochflexiblen Arbeitszeitarrangements', *WSI Mitteilungen*, 54 (October), pp. 626–31.

Rapoport, R. and L. Bailyn (1996) *Relinking Life and Work: Toward a Better Future* (New York: Ford Foundation).

Sato, H. (2000) *The Current Situation of 'Family-friendly' Policies in Japan* (Tokyo: Japan Institute of Labour).

Sato, H. (2001) 'Is "Atypical Employment" a Flexible Form of Working Life?', *Japan Labour Bulletin*, 40 (4).

Schulten, T. (2001) *Agreements signed on Volkswagen's 5000 x 5000 project* (www.eiro.eurofound.ie/print/2001/feature/DE0109201F.html).

Seifert, H. (1993) 'Ausmaß und Effekte der Arbeitzeitverkürzung', in P. Hampe (ed.), *Zwischenbilanz der Arbeitzeitverkürzung* (Munich: Hase & Koehler).

Seifert, H. (2003) 'Paradigm Shift in Working Time Policy through Working Time Accounts – from Standard Working Hours to Controlled Flexibility', *WSI Mitteilungen*, 56.

Stille, F. and R. Zwiener (1997) *Arbeits- und Betriebszeiten in Deutschland* (Berlin: Deutsches Institut für Wirtschaftsforschung).

van het Kaar, R. (1999) *Social Partners Agree Framework for Individualising Terms of employment* (www.eiro.eurofound.ie/print/1999/06/feature/NL9906144F.html).

Wenger, J. (2001) 'The Continuing Problems with Part-Time Jobs', Washington, DC: Economic Policy Institute, Issue Brief ab. 155.

Yamakawa, R. (1998) 'Overhaul after 50 Years: The Amendment of the Labour Standards Law', *Japan Labour Bulletin*, 35 (11).

12
Human Resource Management in BASF Japan

Mahito Yamao and Markus Falk

Introduction

This chapter discusses the transition from a seniority-based human resource (HR) system towards a performance- and communication-based system at BASF Japan. It starts with a short description of BASF and its history, and then briefly considers some of the drivers of changes to the company's HR system in Japan. Next four concrete measures that have been introduced to support the changes will be described. Finally, some factors for successful change in HR management will be derived from the lessons learnt at BASF.

BASF Japan

With 140 years of corporate history, BASF is the biggest and most successful chemical company in the world. It employs approximately 82,000 people world-wide and serves customers in more than 170 countries. Production sites are located in 41 countries. In the last 40 years BASF has gradually transformed itself from a German company to a globally operating transnational. The company's first contact with the Japanese market (textile dyes) was in 1888, and by 1890 its partnership activities in Japan accounted for 1.6 per cent of total corporate turnover. After World War II BASF quickly re-established its business relationship with Japan. In 1949 Yamada Shoten and Shibata Shoten founded – in cooperation with BASF – the Color Chemie Trading Company, which took charge of the sale of BASF products as sole importer. With premises in Tokyo and Osaka, this company provided the foundation for the significance BASF enjoys in Japan today. In 1953 BASF became majority shareholder in Color Chemie, and in 1974 it bought the remaining shares and renamed the company BASF Japan Ltd. Since then the latter has been BASF's headquarters in Japan.

BASF now has seven group companies and joint ventures in Japan. The product range consists of performance products (chemical products for improving products in several industries, examples are: textile and leather chemicals, fuel, etc.), plastics and fibres, chemicals, agricultural products and nutritional products. The company has eight production sites and a workforce of about 1200 people. Sales in 2004 amounted to around US$ 1.18 billion.

Human resource management at BASF Japan

A long corporate history also means a long history of managing human resources, and most of the time the company has been managed along Japanese lines. Although there were German expatriate staff, including German presidents, HR matters were left to local employees. While there were good reasons for this, the situation gradually changed from the early 1990s and HRM went beyond purely administrative handling and was developed as a factor in competitive advantage. Three factors accelerated the changes:

- Trends in the Japanese labour market.
- BASF's global restructuring programme 'Fit For the Future'.
- The introduction of BASF's 'Values and Principles' framework.

Each of these will be briefly described below.

Trends in the Japanese labour market

At BASF Japan we can observe two major trends in the Japanese labour market. First, many capable mid-career persons have begun to look for new jobs as a result of company restructuring and/or the declining attractiveness of lifetime employment to high performers. The second, employees' desire for mobility, has risen significantly. Students have become more internationally minded and many have taken the opportunity to study abroad. This has given them much more self-confidence than exhibited by graduates in the past. These labour market trends have presented both opportunities and challenges to BASF. The regular recruitment of new graduates is an important element of staffing policy at BASF Japan. Until recently the large, well-known Japanese companies were the preferred employers for top graduates from the national universities. While this still tends to be the case, more and more of these graduates wish to pursue an international career and are therefore attracted to foreign companies. In the case of BASF, they are attracted by the prospect of being given challenging assignments and responsibility right from the beginning. All such recruits speak good English, which is the corporate language at BASF Japan. Indeed their English tends to be much better than that of existing employees as English was not an important selection criterion in the past. These recruits also bring fresh ideas and are encouraged to give voice to them. Female graduates are particularly attracted to foreign companies as they can expect better career opportunities than in Japanese companies. At BASF capable female graduates have performed very successfully in jobs that were once regarded as the sole preserve of males, such as the post of sales representative.

With regard to recruits, due to the restructuring of Japanese companies it is now possible to recruit top-quality mid-career persons, ranging from professionals in their thirties to senior advisers close to retirement, although some find it difficult to adjust to a non-traditional Japanese corporate culture. As noted above, high performers are looking for new challenges as part of their career development. For these people lifetime employment has become less attractive as it means that promotion and remuneration are based more on seniority than ability and therefore they are willing to change employers at a certain career stage.

At BASF performance is rewarded in a transparent and fair manner and there are many domestic and international career opportunities for key employees. These career opportunities can be a classical management career or the chance to become an expert in a particular field.

The BASF Group's global restructuring programme

The 'Fit for the Future' project is the second crucial factor in the HRM system at BASF Japan. This project fosters entrepreneurial action and freedom on a regional basis. Until June 2001 BASF Japan was one of three separate divisions in the Asia-Pacific region, but in July 2001 it was integrated into the Regional Division East Asia. Under 'Fit for the Future', responsibility for all operations in the region is assigned to business units located in the BASF headquarters in Singapore and Hong Kong. For BASF Japan and its employees this has meant a significant move from relative independence to being an integrated part of the Asia-Pacific group, with cross-border reporting lines and the establishment of international teams. For the employees in Japan it has resulted in more international exposure and cross-border communication. In the case of some employees, their superiors are no longer in Japan but in Hong Kong or Singapore.

The 'Values and Principles' framework

In early 1999 BASF began to develop a set of values and principles that would apply to the whole group and serve as the cornerstones of the corporate culture and the company's. There are six values, each with its own guiding principles. They are mandatory for all the group's companies and all employees throughout the world. The values and some selected guiding principles that have had a strong influence on HRM activities are:

- Sustainable profitable performance.
  Principle: 'We provide our employees with compensation and benefits based on local market conditions and on individual as well as company performance. Thereby, our working conditions are in compliance with internationally recognized fundamental labour standards'
- Innovation in the service to our customers.
- Safety, health and environmental responsibility.
- Personal and professional competence.
  Principle: 'Our future leaders are promoted preferably from within BASF. The executive team is recruited, selected, developed and positioned systematically based on the following four criteria: knowledge, skills, leadership competencies and conduct in accordance with our Values and Principles.'
- Mutual respect and open dialogue.
  Principle: 'Goals, priorities and responsibilities are mutually agreed upon by managers and their employees or teams.'
  Principle: 'We encourage entrepreneurial initiative by means of appropriate empowerment. Managers discuss with their employees, on a regular basis, their on-going development and encourage their commitment to continuous learning.'
- Integrity.

The principles listed above have had a significant impact on HRM at BASF Japan.

Consequences for the HRM system

It is clear from the preceding discussion that the developments at BASF posed challenges to the HRM system and that changes had to be made. The areas most affected were performance management and human resource development. Support was given to employees in facing these changes, especially the transformation of BASF Japan from a local company to an integrated part of the group's Asia-Pacific operations. Some of the related measures will be discussed below.

The new challenges faced by Human Resources could only be success-fully faced by establishing a powerful HR organization which is clearly interlinked with the business divisions. BASF Japan took care of that by creating a central HR service platform for all group companies in Japan and by establishing a career development committee (CDC), which consisted of the president of BASF Japan, the business directors, the corporate services director and the HR director. Since then all major HR initiatives have had to be presented to and approved by the CDC. The feedback obtained from the CDC ensures that the activities and efforts of the HR team are kept on the right track.

The performance management system

Taking the developments inside and outside BASF Japan into considera-tion, it became obvious that the HR department could not keep up with the requirements and expectations of the company if it retained the seniority-based remuneration system. Thus in the late 1990s BASF Japan started a 'performance partnership' project. This included an evaluation of every job, the reduction of organizational layers and the alignment and streamlining of titles within the company. A 'management by objectives' system was introduced throughout the company. The employees were systematically trained in making effective use of the system by means of what was dubbed an 'employee dialogue'. The basics of this were:

- How to describe the main tasks of a job.
- How to define targets for a job.
- How to assign competences to a job.
- How to assess the main tasks, targets and competences.
- How to feed back the results of these assessments to the employees.
- How to use feedback as a constructive learning opportunity.

Redesigning the remuneration system was another major step in meeting the performance orientation of the company. The introduction of a variable component into the system meant that a bonus pool had to be created. This was done by freezing the basic pay of all employees for three years in order to establish and feed the pool. With the addition of bonus payments to the basic pay the total cash compensation received by employees who met performance expectations did not change, those who outperformed received more money, and those who did not meet the requirements received less money.

The performance management system was further systemized and fine-tuned in 2002, when BASF introduced a single performance management system throughout the Asia-Pacific region. Most of the elements of the system in Japan were included. The principal element of the Asia-Pacific performance management concept was the integration of the Asia-Pacific competence framework. To manage HR development and performance all over the region a set of competences was introduced. These competences were derived from the values and principles framework and were considered crucial in distinguishing BASF from its competitors and essential to its future success.

To promote understanding of the importance of the competences, meetings on the subject were held in all locations and articles were placed on the corporate web and in the corporate newsletter. Thirty workshops were held for the employees of BASF Japan and other group companies to retrain them in performance management and familiarize them with the concept and content of the competences, their assessment and their importance for human resource development. The workshops also provided an excellent opportunity to make all employees aware of the performance management cycle, its deadlines and connections with other elements of the HR system, especially HR development and training activities.

The workshops received mainly positive feedback from the participants and are now included in the induction programme for new employees. They are also used to prepare for the employee dialogue each year and are offered to those who want to refresh their knowledge or discuss with colleagues their experience of employee dialogue and performance management.

In the meantime the salary system has undergone a further step towards performance-related pay. The largest change was shifting part of the fixed (seasonal) bonus to the variable bonus. Total remuneration consisted of 12 months' basic salary plus 2.5 months' basic salary as fixed summer bonus and 2.5 months' basic salary as fixed winter bonus. For the higher job grades (those jobs with the largest scope), part of the fixed bonus was converted to a variable bonus:

- For grade 5 (the highest upper-management grade): three months' salary.
- For grade 4: two months' salary.
- For grade 3: one months' salary.

This change has allowed the company to achieve its goal of variabilizing more than 25 per cent of the annual payment for the highest grade jobs (senior executive managers are excluded as they come under the global remuneration system for senior executives).

The HR development system

The HR development programmes at BASF Japan address the needs of management and employees and prepare them to face the challenges imposed by change. The aim is to increase the number of candidates for local and regional management positions. The highest priority is and will continue to be to help middle managers provide leadership that is inspiring and empowering rather than dictating and report producing. This includes training, development and the selection of the right candidates to fill middle management positions later on.

New graduates: recruitment and integration

BASF's HR development activities start with finding the right recruits for the future of the company. The importance of university graduate recruitment has already been discussed. In recent years the company has developed a systematic approach to targeting specific groups of students; that is, internationally minded students studying business administration or related subjects or chemistry or related subjects. A good command of English is essential.

The associated measures include a recruitment web page, a link with the leading recruitment agency in Japan, and a simple but attractive brochure. The selection procedure has been made easier by holding company seminars at universities or job fairs and carrying out follow-up interviews immediately after the events.

In addition the company has established two types of internship. Internships are not common in Japan and are unknown to most students. The few that exist are viewed more as a contribution to society than a prerecruitment measure. A normal internship in a Japanese company lasts about two weeks, during which time the intern is briefly attached to different departments and receives explanations and presentations by the company, but does no real work.

Under BASF's international internship programme, chemistry students recommended by certain professors are offered an internship in research at BASF's headquarters in Ludwigshafen, Germany. The internship lasts six to eight weeks. Under the domestic internship programme, students serve a four to eight weeks internship at BASF Japan, mainly in commercial departments.

All the recruitment activities described above are designed to convey the image of an open, modern employer that offers a challenging environment from the start of a career. New recruits are assigned to jobs that have been agreed upon during the interview stage of the recruitment process. The first step of the latter consists of an interview with an HR officer to check the student's general suitability for the company and establish his or her special areas of interest. The second interview involves contact with the directors and managers of the business areas in which the student has expressed an interest. This interview process, the assignment of recruits to predetermined jobs and giving them responsibility right from day one distinguishes BASF from its domestic competitors, where recruits still normally start with extensive training and/or rotational programme.

As recruits have not usually had any practical experience, strong support is needed to integrate them into the company. Each recruit has a designated coach who is responsible for their on-the-job training, including setting up and supervising the training plan for the first year. This plan is discussed with the HR department before implementation. Progress is constantly monitored by all parties: The HR department, the coach and the new employee. In addition a senior management mentor takes care of the new employee and provides guidance from a more general perspective. The HR department coordinates this programme and provides networking opportunities – for example a monthly meeting and 'start seminars'. In the monthly meetings directors are invited to provide an overview about the division they are responsible for, the new graduates introduce their work to their fellow newcomers, HR personnel provide information on the HR system and learning opportunities such as business case studies. The start seminars consist of:

- Information days, at which recruits are given a general overview of BASF and meet senior managers.
- Plant training to familiarize the participants with shift work in a chemical plant.
- Problem-solving workshop: new recruits are asked to investigate an issue of importance to the company and are given eight to ten months to come up with a report and a suggestion as to how to improve the situation. The assignment is accompanied by three training elements: project management, presentation skills and effective meetings.
- Career review.

Career development workshop

Once recruits are integrated, steps are taken to identify those with future management potential. A policy that promotes internal promotion rather than hiring outsiders for management positions has to be supported by suitable instruments and have the support of senior managers.

The career development workshop (CDW) is a 'top down' approach. Candidates are nominated by the divisional head according to clearly defined criteria. Final approval for participation is given by the career development committee. The aim of the CDW is to identify potential among high performers and provide them with a learning opportunity. The workshop activities consist of exercises dealing with leadership and communication. It is also based on BASF competences. Observers are directors and outside consultants. The CDW has the following target:

- To generate new performance data in order to select candidates for development in a fair manner.
- To evaluate candidates' current proficiency as an indication of future leadership potential and identify their strengths and developmental needs.
- To give the candidates the opportunity to learn through first-hand experience of leadership tasks and to become aware of their own strengths and developmental needs.
- To motivate each candidate to engage in personal development.

As English is the corporate language and mandatory for all future leaders of BASF world-wide the CDW is conducted in English. However Japanese explanations are available if needed.

All participants receive an information kit prior to the workshop to reassure them that the CDW is about personal development only. In addition an information session with HR personnel is offered. Recently details of the more complex exercises have been issued beforehand so that the participants can familiarize themselves with the contents and make preparations.

The CDW is not an isolated workshop; rather it is embedded in the overall development process. Some features of the process are as follows. Once a year all the directors propose candidates to the career development committee. This proposal has to be substantiated by clearly defined performance criteria. The committee then decides whether each pro- posed candidate should be invited to the CDW or nominated as a local or regional development candidate. After the CDW an individual feedback meeting is held with each candidate, leading to a mutually agreed and signed development plan. The feedback is not only about the workshop but also covers past performance. In the meeting the candidate's development status is fully disclosed and explained. All participants in the development process are discussed once a year by the career development committee and their development plans are checked. Directors are asked to outline the developmental activities engaged of all candidates in their division.

A total of seven workshops were held in 2002 and 2004, and both management and the participants have expressed satisfaction with them. The participants feel that something positive has been accomplished and that the company is taking their development seriously. The results have been accepted as the basis of future individual career planning. It has also been found that the exercises are a good preparation for regional meetings, at which BASF Japan employees unfortunately do not always participate as actively as other Asian colleagues, thus conveying a wrong image.

An interesting spin-off from the CDW has been the establishment of a career path for experts. Some participants are known to be experts in their field; however they find personnel management difficult or are not interested in it. The workshops have revealed to employee and employer that the former might not be a management talent, but as their expertise is crucial to the company an alternative to the classical management career has had to be created.

The expert career approach is designed to help retain key knowledge within the company and to motivate those concerned. It also shows that promotion in the organization does not have to be associated with eventual appointment to a management position. All those who embark on this path must satisfy the following preconditions:

- Outstanding expertise/knowledge that is difficult to acquire from outside.
- Internal and external recognition.
- Excellent BASF know-how.
- Experience of networking with leading external institutes or partner companies.
- The ability to explain their area of expertise to non-experts.

The hurdles are set deliberately high to ensure that expert career paths enjoy a high standing and that those following them are able to represent the company.

Upward feedback

To support its focus on improving leadership quality and encouraging open dialogue within the company, in 2001 BASF introduced 'upward feedback' – the appraisal of superiors by subordinates. The process had been designed by BASF in Germany and it soon became clear that Japan-specific elements were required. The initiative was revolutionary in that it did not fit easily into Japanese culture, which is largely hierarchical.

While upward feedback was not very common in Asia as a whole, it had already been introduced by a few other companies in Japan. In the BASF community in Asia, however, BASF Japan was acting as a pioneer.

To inform employees of the reasons for the introduction of upward feedback a communication was posted on the corporate web:

> The first purpose is *personal development* for people in leadership positions. This instrument provides valuable feedback and gives hints for improvement of the leadership competence and the existing culture within a team. Secondly upward feedback serves as a *communication instrument* to discuss improvement measures for co-operation in organizational units and teams. It embodies a unique chance to discuss issues relating to leadership, cooperation and communication from a different perspective. Often these issues are not discussed in normal day-to-day business. This bottom up approach is an ideal addition to the top down approach of our performance management system. Thus it is another dimension of our open communication system.
>
> In a nutshell upward feedback should
>
> • improve leadership competence
> • improve teamwork and cooperation
> • create a cooperative culture
> • further strengthen open communication.

The main components of the upward feedback process were:

• Interviews with senior managers.
• Meetings on the purpose of upward feedback, attended by all those involved.
• A questionnaire.
• Analysis of the results and preparation of feedback reports.
• Individual feedback session with the appraised manager.
• Team feedback session on the results.
• Joint feedback session with team and manager.

Upward feedback was designed as a joint project by the HR department and an independent external consultancy firm. The selection of the right consultant was crucial. Time was taken to make the selection, based on predefined criteria. Although presentations were made by some 'big names' in the field, BASF chose a very small firm that was highly experienced in feedback processes and was by far the most flexible and least dogmatic. Responsibilities were allocated as follows: the HR department designed the upward feedback process and acted as the process driver, while the consultant took charge of implementation and evaluation.

The process started with the consultants interviewing senior managers. Based on these interviews the questionnaire was finalized. It was clear that this instrument would only work if senior managers acted as role models. All senior managers, who at that time included Japanese, German and American nationals participated in the pilot.

Together with the consultants, the HR department held a general introductory and explanatory session for all the participants (evaluators and evaluated) in the survey. To make sure that everybody participated, sessions were held in all locations. It was explained that participation would be anonymous and the participants would not have to write their names on the questionnaire, which would be sent directly to the consultancy firm rather than the HR department. It was also made clear that upward feedback would have no link to performance appraisal – it would merely be about feedback and dialogue and would be used exclusively for personnel and organizational development purposes.

After the questionnaires were completed the consultancy firm analyzed the results. The firm was also in sole charge of the ensuing feedback sessions on the results. Individual feedback was given to the assessed manager by a consultant, who explained and discussed the results with the manager. Afterwards possible development measures were defined and areas of improvement were derived from the results.

The second part of the process was an information session for the evaluated manager's team. Here too the results were explained and discussed. The team then prepared for their feedback session with their manager by isolating the most important topics to discuss with the latter. Finally, a session was held for all the participants to talk about the results and come up with a joint action plan on improvement that could be made. This session was chaired by the consultant, who ensured that the proceedings were conducted constructively and were not dominated by the manager.

Following the completion of upward feedback for senior managers, almost all middle managers participated in the second round. They were divided into two groups and the sessions were finalized at the end of 2002. In total 11 directors and 53 middle managers from all over the company participated. The whole project took about 20 months.

Follow-up activities have proven to be a little difficult here and there. Some managers have not been willing to discuss their results with their subordinates or to take the measures agreed with the consultants. However the majority have complied, despite the fact the guaranteed confidentiality of the results meant they could not be forced to do so. Senior managers and the majority of middle managers now include upward feedback in their dialogue with employees and use it as input for their development discussions with subordinates and their superiors.

The process has opened the eyes of many participants and provided an excellent analysis of training needs at the company level. A general training programme, based on the most urgent improvement requirements has been designed in partnership with the consultancy firm. It consists of three modules:

- Basic management and planning.
- Effective communication styles.
- Coaching skills.

This programme, which was launched in April 2003, is mandatory for all newly appointed managers at BASF Japan.

As mentioned earlier, one element of the seminars for new recruits is the problem-solving workshop. The topic of this in 2002/3 was 'Evaluation of upward feedback'. In the May career development committee meeting the recruits presented their findings. They proposed improvements and passed on their finding that more than 73 per cent of employees and more than 88 per cent of managers wanted upward feedback to be a permanent cornerstone of the culture of open dialogue in BASF Japan.

Conclusion

BASF Japan has introduced a number of instruments for personnel development and performance management. These are designed to promote open dialogue that transcends hierarchical and departmental borders, as specified in the company's values and principles, and to reduce the *uchi* mentality (the traditional preference of the Japanese to communicate only within their own small group) that still exists to some extent in the company. These instruments include:

- Management by objectives, employee dialogue and performance-related pay.
- New graduate recruitment and integration programmes.
- Career development workshops.
- Upward feedback.

Of course all these initiatives have had teething problems and there have been some setbacks. However valuable lessons have been learnt about successful HR management in Japan and elsewhere.

- Strategic justification: all human resource initiatives must be in line with the corporate vision and/or strategy.
- Transparency: The HR department must overcome its 'corporate police' image if it is to inspire the trust it needs from employees. Trust is essential to making new initiatives a sustainable part of the HR system and not just a one-shot exercise.
- Proper two-way communication: at communication meetings there must be opportunities for employees to voice their concerns. HR personnel must learn to listen carefully to employees and act as communication channels between employees and management.
- Credible implementation: The company must do what it says it is going to do. If difficulties arise they should never be hidden.
- Ensure that the HR department is acting in line with business needs, for example by forming a joint committee.
- Senior management support: senior managers must act as role models and demonstrate that they stand behind all initiatives.

At BASF Japan significant progress has been made in changing management practices and employees are becoming convinced of the necessity of change in the interest of their own career development. The reaction by younger employees has been especially encouraging. They are speaking up more and more and expressing their own opinions. Thus it is not surprising that the proposal to conduct upward feedback came from younger people. The question they asked was very simple: 'We are evaluated regularly by our bosses, so why are we not given the opportunity to evaluate them as well?' This is a very radical question in Japan and demonstrates the speed of the changes taking place among the younger generation in the country, despite media reports to the contrary.

13
Recruitment in Japan

Frank Schulz

Introduction: successful recruiting as a key to the Japanese market

Until today most Japanese companies have believed their employees to be loyal and have not considered fluctuation a major problem. However, the economic crisis is now causing fundamental problems and deregulation, downsizing, and turnover of staff are attacking the tradition of life-long employment and seniority-based payment.

Japanese employees are normally trained in a system of job rotation, sometimes on a long-term basis, which makes them loyal generalists. It has been quite normal for a manager to tie his personal faith and life plan to the same company.

The new generation of managers who are more interested in their own careers, in success-related pay and quality of life are finding it easier to accept change. They observe on a daily basis the ease with which their older superiors are released or how managers of their own age are being thrown on the streets after their companies have been shut down.

Looking for ways to avoid this has made the Japanese more open to alternative approaches to having a career, and changes in employment do not carry the same sort of stigma as they did several years ago. Individual career planning supported by executive search firms, temporary staffing and employment agencies, newspaper or internet-based job advertisements etc. are reaching a higher level of acceptance every day. Alternative employment options – which will be not discussed here – such as job-sharing, part-time work and overseas employment are part of the same approach.

Though finding a job can be difficult these days, many young people, mid-term careerists and even senior managers welcome the new environment and the opportunities it provides. However the majority of older workers are bewildered at the pace of change and frightened by the prospect of a broken lifetime covenant and the looming possibility of unemployment. Under the influence of weaker local competition, positive exchange rates and an open, deregulated market it has become easier for foreign companies to establish businesses in Japan. Every one of these companies is competing to attract suitable and qualified staff.

According to a 'Questionaire Survey on Employment in Foreign Companies in Japan' conducted by the Japanese External Trade Organization (JETRO) in 2002, there are 4190 foreign-owned or affiliated head offices and 1464 other places of foreign business established in Japan. From these figures, JETRO extrapolated a total of 1,006,439 Japanese full-time employees working for these companies which represents 2.3 per cent of a total labour force of 43.2 million. In 60 per cent of all foreign-owned or affiliated head offices and in 40 per cent of other foreign businesses, the staff is 100 per cent Japanese.

The distribution of Japanese employees in foreign companies is as follows: manufacturing industry, 56.4 per cent; wholesale and retail, 13.6 per cent; financial institutions and insurance, 13.5 per cent; other professional services, 12.7 per cent; others 3.8 per cent.

Unfortunately not every Japanese manager looking for a job change offers the qualifications required to be a successful part of a Western company. Foreign language skills, e.g. English are fundamental prerequisites for this kind of employment. Furthermore candidates need the ability to manage the leap between different cultural situations – from a traditional cooperatively organized Japanese firm to a Western company.

A Japanese candidate for a top position not only needs to be able to manage his company's business in Japan, he is also expected to report directly to headquarters in an appropriate manner. Furthermore, the individual must be in a position to offer the following: the ability to prepare and realize business plans; knowledge and understanding of Western decision-making processes; good interpersonal communication skills in teamwork with the foreign management and the ability to work more effectively, more target-oriented and faster. Japanese managers with these prerequisites are of great value to a company but are a rare species!

It is a fact that the demand for qualified employees is substantially higher these days than the labour supply – the dilemma of an employment market with an unemployment rate of 4.6 per cent (June 2004). Even experts think that an unofficial rate of nearly 10 per cent is possible.

In contrast to their Western counterparts, most Japanese companies did not use the last ten years to implement new management concepts and strategies. The orientation of human resource management towards ethnical diversity and qualitative variety in employees is more irrelevant. There are programs to promote women but they are only on a low level and still do not meet with approval socially.

Without fresh ideas there is a risk that the pool of potential employees will remain static in the future. Japanese companies could implement a solution if they started hiring foreigners for middle and higher management positions. Another solution would be time-consuming and costly – training and educating junior managers from international companies in or outside Japan.

A third solution, which some Japanese universities have already implemented, is the establishment of part-time programs for MBA studies. This is one good sign that the need for individual career planning is already being recognized in Japanese society.

The purpose of this chapter is to provide some information on the subject of Japanese recruiting and hiring methods and their cultural singularities. Against the background of transition which could be described best with the phrase 'it has been, it still is and it will be' the reader will be introduced to University Hiring and Mid-Career Hiring.

The transformation of the employment system

The Japanese employment system was and still is partially characterized by lifelong employment and seniority-based compensation and promotion within a single company. The normal Japanese employee expects to stay with one company or family of companies for life and the employer expects that employee to remain throughout his working life.

This results in the development of in-house HR capital on a long-term basis, very strong corporate identity and loyalty in the work force, a wide range of experience and responsibilities via job rotation for the employees and good will on the part of the job applicants especially among university graduates.

Tangible advantages of this system are that employees are guaranteed certain salary levels and employment security. The employer himself is assured that his work force will stay with him for a long period, that fluctuation is limited and that he can safely invest in training his employees, achieving an increase in productivity, but at the same time avoiding the departure of the employee along with the fruits of his investment.

On the other hand, the same system has remarkable economical disadvantages: a poorly developed external employment market, which is focused instead on school and university graduates; hidden below capacity employment in companies; mismatch of the supply and demand of qualified workers externally and internally; pressure on income and profits in times of economic crisis; removal of management flexibility; putting the company before the job; limitation of individual qualifications and unchallenged exclusion of female employees.

Nevertheless the system is in transition from a focus on lifelong employment to a lifelong career orientation. In recent years there has been a tendency to a more Westernized approach in the Japanese labour market which is expressing itself in a more mobile workforce, more merit-based compensation systems, identification of companies as providers of qualifications to further careers and a focus on individual career planning.

University recruiting

Japanese universities, which educate 40 per cent of all high school leavers, are still potentially the most popular source of new recruits to Japanese companies. Even in times of change students very much prefer to join a prestigious Japanese company.

In comparison with foreign-affiliated companies in Japan local companies have been recruiting from universities for a long time and have even managed to establish relationships with professors, university managers and to build their own alumni networks which put them in an advantageous position. It is also customary to make charitable cash and in-kind donations to the universities. This plays an important role in developing and maintaining recruiting relationships.

Japanese companies usually have employees called mediators whose sole responsibility is to recruit from universities and encourage representatives from in-house line functions to participate in the selection process and to maintain contact with their former alma mater and act as tutors. Born out of relations grown over generations there is a strong personal network among companies and universities. Nevertheless all Japanese companies are facing competition when it comes to hiring promising young graduates – especially in the field of engineering and other technical subjects.

A Japanese student normally joins the job hunt, called *'shushokukatsudo'*, in his fourth and final year at university. Around this time, most students are approached, for example by one of the big recruiting firms in

Japan which send out information about job openings. The students then have to apply for the positions they are interested in, using a post-card to ask for more detailed information. Nowadays, more and more students are using speculative applications in response to newspaper or magazine advertisements or replying directly to internet job postings by companies and job agencies. Others are recommended by their professors and those supported by existing alumni get in direct contact by phone or sometimes visit a company right away. In order to learn more about a particular company and what kind of job openings are available, they also attend company sponsored forums or job-fairs organized by companies, local institutions and national and international Chambers of Commerce and Industry.

These events are usually held from March through August. Students are getting in contact with different companies and can make an appointment for a further interview or undertake a screening test if that is company practice.

Another valuable source are the university career centers where every enrolled student – even foreign ones – can get information about full- and part-time job vacancies.

The formal selection and assessment process is conducted between July and November. Most Japanese companies conduct a series of inter-views in which not only HR personnel but also representatives of line functions are present. In the selection process, the applicants attend three or four interviews, each time facing the next level in the hierarchy of line functions and management until the successful candidates reach the final interview with senior management and a decision is made. The students chosen will begin their career with the employer in the April of the following year. An inauguration ceremony takes place on the very first day to encourage them to identify with the company.

Japanese employers are looking for ambition, adaptability and proper social behaviour in new student recruits. All of these attributes should be acquired through school and university education and the inevitable club activities a student has to participate in at every Japanese educa-tional institution. A proper family background and references are also very valuable. Because most Japanese companies are still providing long-term on-the-job training the gathering of work pre-experience like internships, work experience, language proficiency or an MBA are not prerequisites for being hired.

It is very important that foreign companies intending to recruit from universities keep all these unfamiliar customs in mind, develop an approach strategy and pay close attention to students and their professors.

Mid-career and executive hiring

A normal Japanese employee will not leave his employer unless a personal or professional problem occurs. This applies today in bigger Japanese companies. Small and medium-sized companies have always had to make some effort to attract suitable employees.

However since the days of economic downturn and the increased appearance of foreign companies in the Japanese market, a change in employment is not regarded as negatively as in previous years. Nevertheless the so-called 'mother-in-law factor' as a cultural singularity should not be underestimated. The social environment will impact heavily on every decision a future applicant wants to make.

The reasons for change and the expectations of a career at a foreign company are highly individual. Here are some examples of reasons, not in any particular order: higher pay; shorter working hours; sexual equality; objective promotion prospects; objective performance reviews; business trips abroad, a more individual approach to responsibility; a prestigious title and secure employment. Fewer social or cultural obligations in a foreign working environment and the size and reputation of the hiring company are also motives.

An innovative product portfolio, advanced technology, exciting design and research developments influenced by foreign standards are also attractive for Japanese job seekers especially in some industrial and technology branches like automotive, machinery or healthcare.

A future employer should pay more attention to the applicant's abilities, experience, knowledge, character and qualifications than to traditional considerations. Furthermore, hiring companies do not have to invest as much time and money in training or education as in the case of school or university graduates.

Nearly every foreign company in Japan relies heavily on Japanese staff in mid career and on managers and executives, all hired locally. Newcomers to the Japanese market in particular have an urgent need for experienced personnel to ensure their economic success.

To reach a high level of loyalty in the workforce and to remain attractive in the competition for applicants, a foreign company in Japan should give clear statements regarding its character and intention to remain in the Japanese market in the long term. Showing reliability means it will be accorded greater trust and helps to abolish overhasty prejudices. The company should be aware that hiring employees from related companies or even customer companies without approbation is not approved behaviour in the Japanese business community. Nevertheless an inter-company dispatch of workforce between two related companies or customer companies on time-limited project basis is.

The sources from which to acquire mid-career employees are the same as in the rest of the modern business world: personal contacts, networking, newspaper and magazine advertisements, job sites on the Internet, temporary staffing agencies, contingency personnel consulting firms and retained executive headhunters.

The following section introduces some of these sources:

Newspaper advertisements

Unlike the rest of the world newspaper advertisements for job vacancies are quite an underdeveloped source for job hunters in Japan. This especially is the case when it comes to the size of the advertisement and the information content.

With an average measurement of 7 cm × 7.5 cm, the space for information about the hiring company and the vacant position is limited. Furthermore, the hiring company has to pay an average of USD 5,000 to 8,000 for this kind of appetizer.

Placement agencies usually place the advertisement. The agency is then in charge of the layout and contact with the newspapers. Two national newspapers which have advertisements on certain days are the *Nikkei Shinbun* and *The Japan Times*, a daily paper in English.

Internet job pages

Since the mid-1990s the worldwide web has become more and more important in bringing job seekers and hiring companies in Japan together on a daily basis. Even if the Internet never can replace personal contact it is and will be in the future one of the main portals for human resources networking.

There are about 20 to 30 different web sites offering their support in finding a new professional challenge or advertising job vacancies. Some of these sites are international with a Japanese section, some are wholly Japanese. There are both general and specialist search sites organized by branch or by qualification. Especially for job seekers who can record their curricula vitae and other personal information most of these sites are useable at no charge. Hiring companies have to pay a certain amount to place their advertisements. It is estimated that about 600,000 to 700,000 people access these sites frequently.

Temporary staffing agencies

After clarifying their corporate customers' requirements, temporary staffing agencies send them clerical and similar staff on their registers for a limited period of time. Since implementation of the 'Personnel Dispatching Law' in 1986 employers have been allowed to hire such staff for a maximum of one year. After this time the contract can be renewed for a further year. The law requires companies to obtain approval from the Labor Ministry before entering into this kind of arrangement.

After three liberalizations (1999, 2000 and 2003), which have removed most restrictions on the type of job, it is now possible to hire staff from 27 professions (for example, IT, advertising, clerical functions, design, retail etc.). Since March 2004 even the healthcare sector has been covered by the dispatching law.

The agencies charge fees for their services which can be divided into daily, weekly or monthly instalments depending on the period of deployment. A percentage of this fee goes to the worker as salary.

The number of licensed agencies reached a total of 7347 in fiscal year 2001 with 450,000 employees 'dispatched'. According to the latest figures available for dispatched workers in a report on temporary staffing services published by the Ministry of Health, Labor and Welfare in February 2003, there were 2,129,654 temporary workers employed at approximately 360,000 enterprises in fiscal year 2003.

After a preset probationary period and payment of a commission, the hiring company has the option of employing the temporary worker on a permanent basis (temp-to-perm program). This makes the risk of hiring qualified people more manageable for employers and gives Japanese employees the opportunity to gather experience and see if they want to work for a foreign company.

Personnel consulting firms

According to the Japan Executive Search & Recruitment Association (JESRA) there are also around 400 firms and around 1000 offices active in the Japanese placement market which is focusing only on headhunting and recruiting for specialist and executive positions. The total number of government authorized offices handling recruitment matters may be about 2500. These organizations are of different sizes, some with a specific orientation and might be branches of international groups or totally local entities.

The quality of service these firms provide depends very much on the qualifications of their consultants and differs from firm to firm.

Appealingly laid out advertising material or websites do not necessarily guarantee a good service. Potential clients should always ask for a personal interview with different companies to find a service provider which best meets their needs and which gives a professional impression. Differences in fees and the way projects are handled will become apparent.

In general there are two types of companies: 'retainer' firms and 'contingency' firms. The first category charges from 30 to 35 per cent of the candidate's first year gross income for its service. This consulting fee is charged in three equal installments irrespective of whether the search is successful or not – one third on placing the order, one third on the introduction of short-listed candidates and one third when the successful candidate joins the client's company. Some firms charge on a time-frame-based scheme, such as payment of the first installment on placing the order, with payment of the second and third instalments after 35 and 70 days respectively. Contingency firms differ in that they charge for their work on a success basis and will get around 20 to 30 per cent of the applicant's gross income for the first year at the end of each project.

From an economic point of view a lower consulting fee might be advantageous for the contingency firms but closer examination reveals that selecting their services on price criteria could cause problems. Because these firms work strictly on a success basis most of their time is spent on acquisition. Candidates are found via the Internet or from newspaper advertisements, or their details have already been filed in data-bases. Relatively little time is spent on assessing and profiling the candidates.

On the other hand, fast and apparently cheaper completion of the project is associated with candidates of limited qualifications.

Retainer companies have a different approach to recruiting. Their projects take on average about 3 to 6 months and include a replacement guarantee if the employee introduced should leave the client's company during the probation period. In contrast to the contingency projects they only approach candidates whose qualifications and personality match a specification discussed in advance with the client. A professional assessment of candidates in combination with evaluation of their references forms a part of service as does guidance in contract negotiations with the candidate and help to integrate the employee during the probationary period.

The following list of features should be standard for retainer firms: dedicated projects, scheduling, confidentiality, clear fee structure, off limits consultation which guarantees that no already placed candidate will be approached again for another project or that companies are untouchable which are in business relationship to client and for international firms, standardized execution of projects.

Contingency projects are more appropriate for recruiting suitable employees for junior positions on a very short term basis. Companies who are looking for employees for mid or higher management positions may be better served by retainer firms, who are more likely to avoid mismatches.

Both kinds of personnel consulting firms should use their sound knowledge of the market and the country to answer questions, even about labour standards and compensation systems. Candidates should be selected sensitively and with respect for the traditional values of loyalty and discretion allowing them to start building a relationship of trust with their future employer.

Conclusion

In these days Japan finds itself in a period of major economic change which already brought economic stagnation, downturn and now an actual phase of revival. Growing competition with world wide players forces Japanese companies to downsize and to rethink their organizational approach to Human Resources Management.

The corporate idea of life-long employment will be more and more replaced by the individual focus of career planning. Competitive recruitment methods followed by the introduction of highly individual remuneration systems will be the key to attract qualified employees.

Foreign companies in Japan are still having a certain protection because they are used to the idea of 'free deal' in which everybody focuses on individual careers. Nevertheless competition in the 'war for talent' is growing in Japan among each other.

The too often heard statement of Japan being a unique market especially when it comes to hiring suitable people acts only as a limited deterrent. It is just a question of how to find and attract the people a company needs to perform. The methods itself can be adapted and appropriately used like many other things. Suitable applicants up to a certain number are in the market and looking for new challenges.

Nevertheless one situation not discussed here is the willingness of foreign companies in Japan or most of their headquarters abroad to understand and accept the commitment. Coming to Japan with the approach to do business here as in the rest of the world and to deal with people like everywhere else is definitely not the first step into success.

Being under high cost and time pressure will harm the image if shown during hiring process. Also the stigma of being seen as a 'hire and fire' company is not easy to lose in a country where the flow of information between groups is normal.

The willingness to accept seen new and growing expectations and the adjustment to the market, showing reliability – which definitely will also be measured by the behaviour of foreign management representatives in Japan and the credit of a long-term strategy are very attractive reasons for a Japanese employee to choose a foreign company for work.

'Give and Take' shall be the motto.

References

Blechschmidt, S. (2000) 'Deutsches Personalmanagement in Japan', in *Japan Analysen Prognosen 02/03-2000* (www.japan.uni-muenchen.de).

Clement, W. and K. Komizo (2003) 'Where is Japan's Financial Services Industry Heading?', *Search-Consult*, 17, pp. 10–11.

Gross, A. (1999) *Japan Recruiting Update* (www.pacificbridge.com).

Jobpilot (2004) *Bewerben in Japan – Bewerbungsregeln und Auswahlprozess* (www.jobpilot.de/content/journal/international/bewerben/jp/regeln.html).

Lloyd, T. (2004) *Negotiating the pitfalls of recruiting business* (www.japantoday.com/e/?content=comment&id=250).

Japan Institute for Labour Policy and Training (2004) Newsletter 09/2004 (www.jil.go.jp/foreign/emm/bi/11.htm).

Schulz, F. (2001) 'Human Resources, Mut zu neuem Engagement, Japans Arbeitsmarkt wird flexibler und bietet neue Chancen fuer westliche Personalplaner', *ASIA BRIDGE*, 12, pp. 32–3.

Schulz, F. (2003) 'Personalrekrutierung in Japan oder wie gewinne ich den "War for Talents"?', *Japan Markt*, 10, pp. 19–20.

Waldenberger, F. (2000) 'Arbeitslosigkeit in Deutschland und Japan, Ein statistischer Vergleich', in *Japan Analysen Prognosen 09/2000* (www.japan.uni-muenchen.de).

Index